W9-BTZ-750

2nd EDITION

Ventures 4

WORKBOOK

rm345

Gretchen Bitterlin Dennis Johnson Donna Price Sylvia Ramirez
K. Lynn Savage (Series Editor)
with Kristin L. Johannsen

CAMBRIDGE
UNIVERSITY PRESS

CAMBRIDGE
UNIVERSITY PRESS

32 Avenue of the Americas, New York, NY 10013-2473, USA

Cambridge University Press is part of the University of Cambridge.

It furthers the University's mission by disseminating knowledge in the pursuit of education, learning and research at the highest international levels of excellence.

www.cambridge.org
Information on this title: www.cambridge.org/9781107661943

First published 2008
2nd printing 2014

Printed in Mexico by Quad / Graphics Querétaro, S.A. de C.V.

A catalog record for this publication is available from the British Library.

ISBN 978-1-107-68157-6 Student's Book with Audio CD
ISBN 978-1-107-66194-3 Workbook with Audio CD
ISBN 978-1-139-88349-8 Online Workbook
ISBN 978-1-107-69841-3 Teacher's Edition with Assessment Audio CD / CD-ROM
ISBN 978-1-107-63513-5 Class Audio CDs
ISBN 978-1-107-61945-6 Presentation Plus

Additional resources for this publication at www.cambridge.org/ventures

Art direction, book design, photo research, and layout services: Q2A / Bill Smith
Audio production: CityVox, LLC

Illustration credits

Chuck Gonzales: 57

Kim Johnson: 47, 71, 104

Q2A Media Services: 2, 3, 5, 29, 45, 53, 62, 65, 77, 78, 82, 89, 95, 101

Monika Roe: 8, 80, 117

Photography credits

Cover front (tl) Andrew Zarivny/Shutterstock, (tr) Stuart Monk/Shutterstock, (r) Gary D Ercole/ Photolibrary/Getty Images, (cr) Sam Kolich, (br) Nathan Maxfield/iStockphoto (c) Monkey Business Images/Shutterstock, (bl) Alistair Forrester Shankie/ iStockphoto, (cl) ML Harris/Iconica/Getty Images, (l) Mark Lewis/Digital Vision/Getty Images, back (tc) cloki/Shutterstock, (br) gualtiero boffi/ Shutterstock

4 (tcl) ©Photofusion Picture Library/Alamy

6 (tr) ©Val Thoemer/Shutterstock

11 (bl) ©Raymond Boyd/Michael Ochs Archives/ Getty Images, (br) ©Yellow Dog Production/Getty images

15 (tl) ©Roxana Gonzalez/Shutterstock

17 (bl) ©Spiderstock/istockphoto, (bl) ©Margo Harrison/Shutterstock, (br) ©Songquan Deng/ Shutterstock, (br) ©blackred/istockphoto

22 (tr) ©Buzz Productions/iStockphoto

24 (cr) ©iStockphoto/Thinkstock

32 (tr) ©Vladimir Wrangel/Shutterstock

36 (tr) ©Sherif A. Wagih/Getty Images

39 (tr) ©Visage/Getty images

43 (tl) ©itanistock/Alamy, (tr) ©kristian sekulic/ iStockphoto

49 (br) ©olson/iStockphoto

66 (tr) ©StockLite/Shutterstock

74 (tr) ©cobalt88/Shutterstock

85 (tr) ©Shmer/Shutterstock

86 (tr) ©Ariadne Van Zandbergen/Getty Images

90 (tr) ©lightpoet/Shutterstock

92 (cr) ©moodboard/Corbis

96 (br) ©Deklofenak/Shutterstock

102 (cr) ©Alex Staroseltev/Shutterstock

106 (tr) ©Roy Morsch/Media Bakery

108 (tr) ©Herbert Kehrer/Corbis

110 (tr) ©Wessel du Plooy/Shutterstock

113 (tr) ©TonyV3112/Shutterstock

114 (tr) ©Andrew Holt/Getty Images

120 (cr) ©Steve Collender/Shutterstock

122 (bcl) ©PhotosIndia.com LLC/Alamy

125 (tr) ©FMB PHOTO/Getty Images

Contents

Welcome

1 Listen to the conversation. Then circle the correct answers.

TRACK 2

1. One of Jin-ho's problems with English is that ____.
   a. he doesn't know how to sing
   b. some people speak too fast
   c. he feels he speaks too slowly
2. When Jin-ho speaks, ____.
   a. people are sometimes impatient
   b. people can't understand him
   c. he gets extremely nervous
3. Jin-ho learns that ____.
   a. singing isn't a good strategy for him
   b. he isn't really serious about singing
   c. singing can help him learn English
4. Jin-ho's English class is now studying ____.
   a. the past continuous
   b. the present continuous
   c. the present perfect continuous
5. When Jin-ho tries to sing a line from a song, ____.
   a. it's too difficult for him
   b. it helps him
   c. he sings it very slowly
6. Jin-ho says that in the future ____.
   a. he'll sing where no one can hear him
   b. he'll sing in his English class
   c. he won't be able to sing in English

Check your answers. See page 135.

2 Complete the story. Use the past continuous or the simple past. Then listen.

TRACK 3

News flash: July 1, Toronto, Canada

Yesterday, at 3:30 p.m. somebody stole (1. steal) Mary Maxwell's purse while she was buying (2. buy) bread at SaveMart. The police talked (3. talk) to three people about the crime.

First, they spoke (4. speak) to Hannah Harding. She said, "Hey, it wasn't me. At 3:30, I was standing (5. stand) in line at the checkout. Ask the cashier. She said (6. say) hello to me."

Next, they interviewed Robby Steel. He said, "I didn't do it. I was leaving (7. leave) the store at 3:15. At 3:30 p.m., I was walking (8. walk) down Second Avenue. I'm sure that no one saw (9. see) me."

The last person was Fred Freeman. He said, "3:30? At that time, I was looking (10. look) for my favorite cereal. The stock clerk helped me find it. He'll remember me."

Who isn't telling the truth? Do you know?

3 Write sentences. Use the simple past and the past continuous.

1. I / read a mystery story /the lights go out

   I was reading a mystery story when the lights went out.

2. Sue / drive down Park Avenue / run out of gas

   Sue was driving down park Avenue when she ran out of gas.

3. The fire / start / we / watch TV

   The fire started. when We were watching TV.

4. They / walk past the car / the car alarm go off

   They were walking past the car when the car alarm went off.

5. The thief / steal the bicycle / the boys play soccer

   The thief stole the bicycle when the boys were playing soccer.

Check your answers. See page 135.

4 Complete the interview. Use the simple past or the present perfect. Then listen.

TRACK 4

Margo is a student at City College, and she works at the college radio station WFCC. Today she's interviewing Jon Redmond. He's an actor in the college theater club.

A Hi, everyone. Today I'm talking to Jon Redmond about the theater club. Jon, __have__ you ever __acted__ (1. act) in any of the club's plays?

B Yes, I have. I __have been__ (2. be) in several plays. Last year, I __played__ (3. play) the part of George Gibbs in the play *Our Town*.

A Yes, now I remember that. I __saw__ (4. see) it and you were great. __Have__ you ever __forgotten__ (5. forget) your lines in a play?

B Yes, I have. I think that happens to everyone. In fact, I __forgot__ (6. forget) some of my lines in *Our Town*.

A Really? I __didn't notice__ (7. not notice) it. What's the most difficult part you __have__ ever __had__ (8. have)?

B Hmm. I was Tony in the musical *West Side Story* two years ago. It __took__ (9. take) me a long time to memorize the words to all the songs. I also __needed__ (10. need) to take singing lessons. But it was a wonderful experience.

Check your answers. See page 135.

5 Read the story. Then complete the questions for the answers.

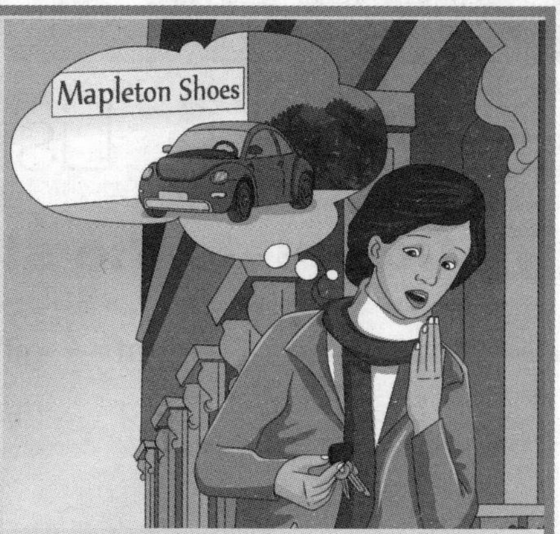

Mariah usually takes the train to work. It takes her about 30 minutes to get to her job at a shoe store in Mapleton. Yesterday, when Mariah was eating breakfast, she heard some news on the radio. It said, "There has been an accident on the train line going to Mapleton. There will be no train service this morning."

So Mariah decided to drive to work. It took her almost an hour to get to work because there was a lot of traffic. Luckily, she was able to park in the company's parking lot. She had a long, hard day at work. When she finally left at the end of the day, she was very tired. She was looking forward to a relaxing ride home on the train. She got to the station and got on the train. She got off the train at her stop and started to walk to her house. She put her hand in her pocket to look for her house keys and suddenly took out her car keys! "Oh, dear!" she said. "I forgot that I drove to work this morning. My car is still in Mapleton. I've never made a mistake like this before. I must be very tired!"

1. How *does Mariah usually get to work*?
   She usually takes the train to work.
2. How long does Mariah usually get to work?
   It takes her about 30 minutes.
3. What was she doing when she heard the news?
   She was eating breakfast.
4. Why did it take her an hour to get to work?
   Because there was a lot of traffic.
5. Where did she park?
   She parked in the company's parking lot.
6. How did she feel at the end of the day?
   At the end of the day, she felt very tired.
7. What did she find in her pocket?
   She found her car keys in her pocket.
8. Where was her Car?
   Her car was still in the parking lot in Mapleton.
9. Has she ever made a mistake like this before?
   No, she's never made a mistake like this before.

Check your answers. See page 135.

UNIT 1 Personal information

LESSON A Listening

1 Complete the story. Then listen.

TRACK 5

aptitude	bright	gifted in	mechanical
brain	fixing	mathematical	musical

My name is Ellen Friedman. I'm an English teacher at Stone Valley Community College. I have 16 students in my class. Each student has a different __aptitude__(1) and is good at different things. For example, Young-mi is very __musical__(2). She plays and sings very well, and she even writes songs. Alicia isn't __gifted in__(3) music, and she can't sing. She's very __mathematical__(4) and takes advanced math classes. David is good at __fixing__(5) things like cars and computers. He's the __mechanical__(6) one in the class. As for Luis, the other students often call him a __brain__(7) because he gets the best scores on all the tests. It's a very interesting class, and I enjoy working with such __bright__(8) students.

2 Circle *T* (True) or *F* (False). Use the information from Exercise 1.

1. Ms. Friedman has 15 students in her class. T F
2. David gets the best scores on tests. T F
3. Young-mi writes songs. T F
4. Alicia is gifted in math. T F
5. David isn't gifted at fixing things. T F
6. Ms. Friedman thinks her students are intelligent. T F
7. Luis is mechanical. T F
8. Alicia is not musical. T F

Check your answers. See page 135.

3 Circle the correct words.

1. Nicholas has no aptitude for art. He **can** / **can't** draw very well.
2. Galina is gifted in math. She usually **wins** / **doesn't win** math contests at school.
3. Jun-ho is the mechanical one in the family. He likes **fixing things** / **writing music**.
4. Esther is very bright. Her grades in school are **good** / **bad**.
5. Hassan is musical. He **can** / **can't** sing very well.
6. Mimi has an aptitude for cooking. She **can** / **can't** make delicious food.

4 Complete the sentences.

aptitude	bright	gifted in	mechanical
brain	fix	mathematical	musical

1. People can be ___gifted in___ many different ways.
2. My brother has ___mathematical___ ability. He's very good with numbers.
3. Irene has an ___musical___ for music and can play three instruments.
4. I'm going to ask a mechanic to ___fix___ my car. It has a lot of problems now.
5. All the people in my family are very ___bright___. We like to sing together.
6. I need to find someone ___mechanical___ who can repair my bicycle. It's not working.
7. Lia is a ___aptitude___ and always gets good grades in her classes.
8. My little sister is very ___brain___. She's four years old, and she can already read.

5 Listen. Then write *Ruth* or *Colin* in each sentence.

TRACK 6

1. ___Colin___ isn't very gifted in math.
2. ___Ruth___ doesn't have a lot of musical aptitude.
3. ___Ruth___ says that people can get better at things if they practice a lot.
4. ___Colin___ remembers that success is 90 percent hard work.

Check your answers. See page 135.

LESSON B Parts of speech

Study the grammar explanation on page 126.

1 Complete the chart.

	Adjectives	Adverbs
1.	perfect	*perfectly*
2.	quick	quickly
3.	skillful	skillfully
4.	good	well
5.	easy	easily
6.	beautiful	beautifully
7.	slow	slowly

2 Look at the pictures. Complete the sentences with the adverb form of the words in the box.

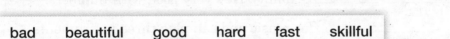

bad	beautiful	good	hard	fast	skillful

1. She dances *skillfully*.

2. He paints beautifully.

3. He works hard.

4. She cooks well.

5. He drives fast.

6. She sings badly.

Check your answers. See page 135.

3 Circle the correct words.

1. Natalie is an opera singer. She sings **professional** / **professionally**.
2. Daniel is a **skillful** / **skillfully** carpenter. He builds new houses.
3. My son speaks English **perfect** / **perfectly**. He has an aptitude for learning languages.
4. I don't like driving very much. I'm a very **slow** / **slowly** driver.
5. I'm a nurse. I always follow directions **careful** / **carefully** at work.
6. Everybody loves that restaurant. The cook is **wonderful** / **wonderfully**.
7. I love that painting! I think you paint very **good** / **well**.
8. Omar has an aptitude for fixing computers. He can fix them very **quick** / **quickly**.

4 Read the chart. Complete the sentences about Sita and Peggy.

	Sita	Peggy
Typing	20 words in a minute (slow)	75 words in a minute (quick)
Cooking	Indian, Mexican, and American food (good)	American food (bad)
Driving	no accidents (careful)	no accidents (skillful)

1. Typing

   Sita ___is a slow___ typist.

   She ___types slowly___.

   Peggy ___is a quick___ typist.

   She ___types quickly___.

2. Cooking

   Sita ___is a good___ cook.

   She ___cooks well___.

   Peggy ___is a bad___ cook.

   She ___cooks badly___.

3. Driving

   Sita ___is a careful___ driver.

   She ___drives carefully___.

   Peggy ___is a skillful___ driver.

   She ___drives skillfully___.

Check your answers. See page 135.

LESSON C Noun clauses

Study the grammar explanation on page 126.

1 Rewrite the sentences. Use *that*.

1. Alicia's teacher thinks she is smart.
   Alicia's teacher thinks that she is smart.
2. I think math is an interesting subject.
   I think that math is an interesting subject.
3. My teacher believes all her students are gifted.
   My teacher believes that all her students are gifted.
4. Do you feel cooking is very important?
   Do you feel that cooking is very important?
5. Do you realize he'll be famous someday?
   Do you realize that he'll be famous someday?

2 Write questions with *that* and a noun clause.

1. People are smart in different ways. (Do you think . . . ?)
   Do you think that people are smart in different ways?
2. Exercising three times a week is important. (Do you agree . . . ?)
   Do you agree that excercising three times a week is important?
3. You have mechanical aptitude. (Does your teacher think . . . ?)
   Does you teacher think that you have mechanical aptitude.
4. All children should learn a second language. (Do you believe . . . ?)
   Do you believe that all children should learn a second language?
5. You have an interesting job. (Do you think . . . ?)
   Do you think that you have an interesting job ?
6. All students should take music classes. (Do you feel . . . ?)
   Do you feel that all students should take music classes?
7. She is gifted in music. (Does she realize . . . ?)
   Does she realize that she is gifted in music ?
8. Tom has interesting friends. (Does he agree . . . ?)
   Does he agree that Tom has interesting friends ?

Check your answers. See page 135.

3 Circle your opinion. Then write sentences with *that* and a noun clause.

1. People are smart in different ways. (**I agree** / **I don't agree**)
   I agree that people are smart in different ways.
2. Women are more interested in taking care of children than men. (**I'm sure** / **I'm not sure**)
   I'm sure that Women are more interested in taking care of children than men.
3. Mathematical skills are important in life. (**I feel** / **I don't feel**)
   I feel that Mathematical skills are important in life.
4. Men like reading more than women. (**I believe** / **I don't believe**)
   I don't believe that men like reading more than women.
5. Women are better at cooking than men. (**I agree** / **I don't agree**)
   I don't agree that women are better at cooking than men.

4 Answer the questions. Use introductory clauses.

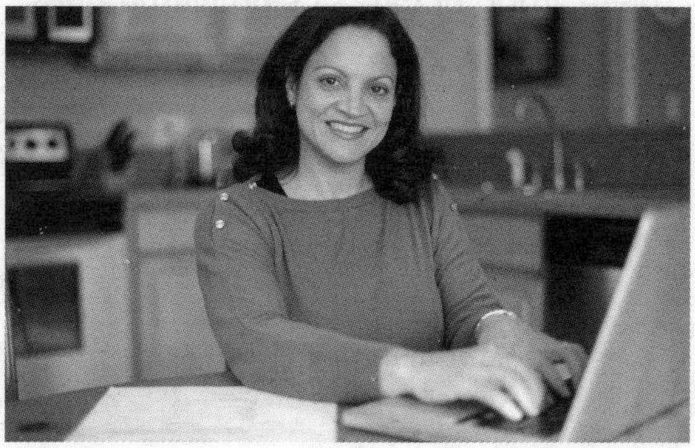

1. Is the singer 25 or 45? (I'm sure . . .)
   I'm sure (that) he's 25.
2. Is he more gifted in music or math? (I'd say . . .)
   I'd say (that) he's more gifted in music.
3. Does he have an aptitude for singing? (I think . . .)
   I think (that) he has an aptitude for singing.
4. Is the woman 30 or 50? (I'd say . . .)
   I'd say (that) she's 50.
5. Is she working in an office or at home? (I think . . .)
   I think (that) she is working in an office.

Check your answers. See page 135.

LESSON D Reading

1 Match the intelligences with the definitions.

1. logical / mathematical f
2. interpersonal g
3. musical / rhythmical e
4. visual / spatial b
5. bodily / kinesthetic c
6. intrapersonal d
7. naturalist h
8. verbal / linguistic a

a. These people like words, reading, and speaking.
b. These people are usually good at drawing and painting.
c. These people learn best when they are moving.
d. These people enjoy spending time alone.
e. These people are sensitive to sound and rhythms.
f. These people like solving logic problems and puzzles.
g. These people easily understand other people.
h. These people like working with plants and animals.

2 Complete the chart.

dance	join a club	take pictures
do math puzzles	play basketball	understand one's own emotions
draw pictures	play the guitar	work with numbers
go to a park	read a book	write in a journal
have a dog or cat	sing with friends	
help other people	spend time alone	

Primary intelligence	Activities
Verbal / Linguistic	1. *read a book* 2. *write in a journal*
Logical / Mathematical	3. do math puzzles 4. work with numbers
Musical / Rhythmical	5. sing with friends 6. play the guitar
Visual / Spatial	7. draw pictures 8. take pictures
Bodily / Kinesthetic	9. play basketball 10. dance
Interpersonal	11. help other people 12. join a club
Intrapersonal	13. spend time alone 14. understand one's own emotions
Naturalist	15. have a dog or cat 16. go to a park

Check your answers. See page 135.

3 Which primary intelligence is the most important for each job? Read and write. Then listen.

TRACK 7

1.

PARK ASSISTANT

Jefferson Park needs an assistant to take care of trees and plants. You will also give nature talks to school classes and families. You must know about all the trees in the park.

2.

ACCOUNT CLERK

Memorial Hospital's accounting department is looking for a careful and reliable clerk. You will prepare and send bills to patients. You must enjoy working with numbers and using computers.

3.

PHOTOGRAPHER FOR *TRAVEL ASIA* MAGAZINE

You will take pictures of people, buildings, and nature in Asia. You must have five years of experience and a strong sense of color and design.

4.

STUDENT COUNSELOR

Do you enjoy helping people? Do you understand people's feelings? Sealand Community College needs a counselor to work with new students. You must have excellent communication skills.

1. naturalist
2. mathematical
3. visual
4. interpersonal

4 Complete the sentences.

interpersonal	kinesthetic	multiple /'mʌltəpəl/ 多種的	visual
intrapersonal	logical	primary /'praimeri/ 主要的	

1. Sports classes in school help children to develop their kinesthetic ability.
2. Rick drives really badly. He has had multiple car accidents.
3. You need good interpersonal skills to work in a big office with many people.
4. Salma is very logical. She thinks about problems very carefully until she finds the answer.
5. Ramesh speaks four languages, but his primary language is English.
6. Intrapersonal means "inside of a person."
7. Many children learn best when they have pictures and other visual information to look at.

Check your answers. See page 135.

LESSON E Writing

1 Read all of the sentences from each paragraph. They are not in order. Mark the topic sentence *T*. Mark the supporting sentences *S*.

Paragraph A

1. __S__ I think that I can draw well, and I have painted pictures of all my friends.
2. __T__ My strongest intelligence is visual.
3. __S__ I love taking pictures of family parties and vacations.
4. __S__ My friends say that I have an aptitude for art.

Paragraph B

1. __S__ I have a lot of plants in my house, and I like taking care of my garden.
2. __S__ When I was growing up, I always had a dog or a cat.
3. __S__ On weekends, I enjoy going to the park or taking a walk on the beach.
4. __T__ I've always loved nature.

2 Read the two paragraphs. Choose the best topic sentence for each paragraph. Write it on the line.

My primary intelligence is interpersonal.	My strongest intelligence is kinesthetic.
My primary intelligence is mathematical.	My strongest intelligence is visual / spatial.

1. My strongest intelligence is kinesthetic. My parents say that I started running before I was two years old. When I was a child, I played soccer every day after school. I don't like to sit down – I always want to move around and be active. I like swimming in summer and playing basketball in winter. My friends think that I have a real aptitude for sports. I learned to play tennis in just a few weeks.

2. My primary intelligence is mathematical. We had very good math teachers at my school, and I really enjoyed their classes. I always got good grades, and I sometimes asked my teachers for extra problems. I enjoyed helping my friends with their math homework. In high school, I won two big math contests for all of the schools in our city. My parents were very proud of me.

Check your answers. See page 135.

3 Read the information about Victor. Complete the outline.

Victor's Profile

- ***Languages:*** Portuguese, Spanish, English
- ***Prizes:*** First prize, National Story-writing Contest, 2011
- ***Hobbies:*** Reading, writing stories

- ***Victor's mother says:*** "He could say long sentences before he was two years old!"
- ***Victor's friends say:*** "He writes really great e-mails!"

My Photo

Topic sentence: *Victor's primary intelligence is verbal / linguistic.*

Supporting details:

- ______
- ______
- ______
- ______
- ______

4 Write a paragraph about Victor's primary intelligence. Use your outline from Exercise 3 to help you.

Victor's primary intelligence is verbal / linguistic.

Check your answers. See page 135.

LESSON F Another view

1 Read the questions. Look at the chart. Then fill in the answers.

Primary Intelligences of High-Intermediate ESL Students at Stone Valley Community College

Intelligence	Number of Students
Bodily / Kinesthetic	4
Interpersonal	12
Intrapersonal	5
Logical / Mathematical	13
Musical / Rhythmical	6
Naturalist	3
Verbal / Linguistic	18
Visual / Spatial	15

1. This chart tells about the ____.
   Ⓐ students' daily activities
   Ⓑ most intelligent students in a class
   ● intelligences of college students
   Ⓓ number of students in different classes

2. Musical intelligence is primary for ____ students.
   Ⓐ 3
   Ⓑ 4
   Ⓒ 5
   Ⓓ 6

3. The primary intelligence of the largest group of students is ____.
   Ⓐ naturalist
   Ⓑ interpersonal
   Ⓒ verbal / linguistic
   Ⓓ bodily / kinesthetic

4. The primary intelligence of the smallest group of students is ____.
   Ⓐ naturalist
   Ⓑ intrapersonal
   Ⓒ visual / spatial
   Ⓓ logical / mathematical

5. Thirteen students have ____ intelligence.
   Ⓐ visual / spatial
   Ⓑ logical / mathematical
   Ⓒ musical / rhythmical
   Ⓓ verbal / linguistic

6. This chart does not have information about ____.
   Ⓐ students' aptitudes
   Ⓑ students who are gifted in mathematics
   Ⓒ students who work well with plants and animals
   Ⓓ the differences between men and women students

Check your answers. See page 135.

2 What does speaker B mean? Circle the answer with a similar meaning.

1. **A** Do you think that you'll get a job at the music store?

   B Yes, I think so.

   a. I really want the job.

   b. I'll probably get the job.

2. **A** Do you think that you'll get a job at the music store?

   B Yes, I hope so.

   a. I really want the job.

   b. I'll probably get the job.

3. **A** Do you think that you will have to take calculus next year?

   B I hope not.

   a. I probably won't take calculus.

   b. I don't want to take calculus.

4. **A** Do you think that you will have to take Spanish next year?

   B I don't think so.

   a. I probably won't take Spanish.

   b. I don't want to take Spanish.

3 What do you think? Answer the questions as in the examples. Use your own ideas.

A Do you think that it's essential to speak two languages these days? (think)

B Yes, I think so. (Or No, I don't think so.)

A Do you think that it will rain tomorrow? (hope)

B I hope so. (Or I hope not.)

1. Do you think that this a beautiful painting? (think)

   No. I don't think so.

2. Do you think that this dress really costs $6,000? (hope)

   No. I hope not.

3. Do you think that you will travel to this place someday? (hope)

   Yes. I hope so.

4. Do you think that Chinese is an easy language to learn? (think)

   No. I don't think so.

Check your answers. See page 135.

UNIT
2 At school

LESSON A Listening

1 Read and answer the questions. Then listen.

TRACK 8

Dear Angela,

I'm really excited about my plans! You know I've been thinking about a new career. I enjoy cooking, and I like meeting new people. So I've decided to study for a certificate in restaurant cooking. I found a new culinary arts program at Rivertown Community College that takes only one year. There are seven required classes and a three-month required internship in a restaurant. After I finish, the school will help me find a job in the restaurant industry.

At first, I wasn't sure about this idea. I talked to a counselor at the college, and I asked a lot of questions. I was worried because the culinary arts program is expensive. Each class is three units, and I have to pay for my books and the kitchen fee, so the cost is more than $1,200. But financial aid is available, and the counselor says I qualify. I was also worried about my English, but the counselor said that there are many bilingual students in the program. The deadline is July 1, but I've already applied! I'm really motivated because I think it will be so interesting, and there are a lot of high-paying jobs in restaurants.

I'll tell you all about my classes next time. Take care!

Love,
Kristina

1. Write two reasons why Kristina wants to work in a restaurant.
   a. *She enjoys cooking.*
   b. *She likes meeting new people.*
2. Write two requirements of the culinary arts program.
   a. ______________________
   b. ______________________
3. Write two things that Kristina was worried about.
   a. ______________________
   b. ______________________
4. Write two things that the counselor told Kristina.
   a. ______________________
   b. ______________________

Check your answers. See pages 135–136.

2 Circle the correct words.

1. Silvia has a high-paying job, so she earns **a lot of / a little** money.
2. A deadline is the **first / last** day that you can do something.
3. If you qualify for something, you **can / can't** have it.
4. If you are bilingual, you speak **two / three** languages fluently.
5. An internship gives you the experience of a type of **work / class**.
6. A requirement is something that you **can / must** do.
7. If you are motivated, you want to **relax / work hard**.

3 Complete the sentences.

bilingual	high-paying	internship	qualify
deadline	industry	motivated	requirement

1. The tourism industry means all the businesses that work with tourists.
2. Jelena is doing a one-month ________ in a restaurant. There's no pay for her work, but she's learning a lot.
3. The ________ for that program is six classes. You have to pass all of the classes.
4. The ________ for registration is next month. You must register before January 15.
5. Cho speaks both English and Korean. She's ________.
6. Frank is very ________ to get a better job. He wants to earn more money and buy a house.
7. Luisa will ________ for financial aid because she has a low income and very good grades.
8. There are some ________ jobs in the tourism industry. You can earn a lot of money.

4 Listen. Then circle the correct answers.

TRACK 9

1. One of the requirements for admission is **experience / a math class**.
2. **Sixteen / Fifteen** classes are required to complete the program.
3. The cost of the mechanic's tools is **$2,250 / $2,000**.
4. Help available for students includes **free tools / paid internships**.

Check your answers. See page 136.

LESSON B The passive

Study the grammar explanation on page 127. For a list of past participles, turn to page 134.

1 Complete the sentences. Use the present passive.

1. My computer class ___is held___ (hold) in the science building.
2. The Hospitality and Tourism Certificate Program ______________ (offer) every year.
3. __________ an English test ______________ (give) to all students?
4. Six classes ______________ (require) for the Hospitality and Tourism Certificate.
5. Where __________ the admissions office ______________ (locate)?

2 Rewrite the sentences. Use the present passive.

1. The college offers job placement services.
   Job placement services are offered by the college.
2. The college requires an English test.
   ____
3. My school provides financial aid.
   ____
4. The teacher checks our homework every night.
   ____
5. The school arranges internships.
   ____

3 Read the sentences. Underline the verbs. Then circle *Active* or *Passive*.

1. English classes <u>are held</u> in the main building. Active (Passive)
2. The college offers financial aid. Active Passive
3. A math test is required for all students. Active Passive
4. Free textbooks are provided for that class. Active Passive
5. The school holds classes at night. Active Passive

Check your answers. See page 136.

4 Read the information. Write questions and answers. Use the present passive.

COURSE SCHEDULE

CUAR 102 Introduction to Food Preparation	CUAR 220 Food Safety
• **Requirement:** Pass math placement test.	• **Requirement:** Pass CUAR 102.
• **Fall and spring**	• **Spring**
• **M / W / F 8:00–10:30 a.m.**	• **T / Th 8:00–10:30 a.m.**
• **Room:** Kitchen (Anderson Building)	• **Online course**

1. when / Introduction to Food Preparation / offer

   A *When is Introduction to Food Preparation offered?*

   B *It's offered in the fall and spring.*

2. is / math placement test / require / for CUAR 102

   A *Is a math placement test required for CUAR 102?*

   B *Yes, it is.*

3. what time / CUAR 102 / offer

   A ______________________________

   B ______________________________

4. where / CUAR 102 / hold

   A ______________________________

   B ______________________________

5. is / Food Safety / offer / in the fall?

   A ______________________________

   B ______________________________

6. is / CUAR 220 / offer / online

   A ______________________________

   B ______________________________

7. what time / CUAR 220 / offer

   A ______________________________

   B ______________________________

Check your answers. See page 136.

LESSON C The passive

Study the grammar explanation and the list of common infinitives after passive verbs on page 127.

1 Read the sentences. Circle the passive verbs. Underline the infinitives.

1. Applicants are required to meet the deadline.
2. Each student is asked to pay a kitchen fee.
3. Students are allowed to take one class online.
4. The teacher is expected to give a test at the end of the term.
5. All of our students are encouraged to meet with a counselor.
6. Students are told to work with a partner in the kitchen.

2 Read the sentences about the Culinary Arts Program. Rewrite them with the present passive and infinitive.

1. We expect new students to come early for registration.
   New students are expected to come early for registration.
2. We require all students to have a health checkup.
   ____
3. We advise some students to enroll in a math class.
   ____
4. We encourage our students to visit restaurants.
   ____
5. We expect all students to have an internship.
   ____
6. We allow many students to earn credits for their jobs.
   ____
7. We tell some students to go to tutoring.
   ____
8. We require our students to take six courses for the certificate.
   ____

Check your answers. See page 136.

3 Read the information about the program. Write conversations. Use the present passive with infinitives.

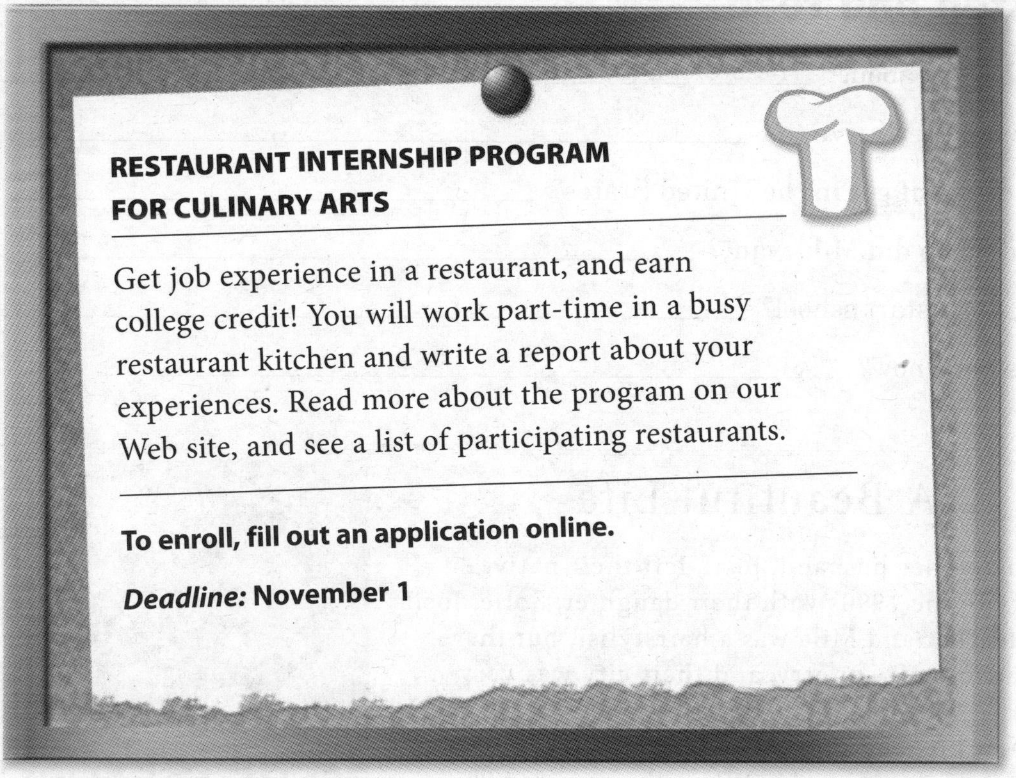
RESTAURANT INTERNSHIP PROGRAM
FOR CULINARY ARTS
Get job experience in a restaurant, and earn college credit! You will work part-time in a busy restaurant kitchen and write a report about your experiences. Read more about the program on our Web site, and see a list of participating restaurants.
To enroll, fill out an application online.
Deadline: November 1

1. **A** *Are all students required to have an internship?*
(all students / require / have an internship)

   B *No, but they are encouraged to get experience in a restaurant.*
(no / they / encourage / get experience in a restaurant)

2. **A** ______________________________
(students / allow / earn credit for the internship)

   B ______________________________
(yes / they / allow / earn up to five credits)

3. **A** ______________________________
(interns / expect / work full-time in the restaurant)

   B ______________________________
(no / they / require / work eight to ten hours a week)

4. **A** ______________________________
(participants / expect / do homework for their internship)

   B ______________________________
(no / they / ask / write a report at the end)

5. **A** ______________________________
(where / students / tell / fill out an application)

   B ______________________________
(students / tell / fill out an application / online)

Check your answers. See page 136.

LESSON D Reading

1 Scan the reading. Answer the questions. Then listen and read.

TRACK 10

1. Who is the story about? *The story is about Mila, Josif, and Sofie.*
2. What city did they move to? ______
3. What job did Josif get in the United States? ______
4. What kind of job did Mila want? ______
5. When did Sofie start school? ______
6. How old is Sofie now? ______

A Beautiful Life

Mila and her husband, Josif, left their native country in the 1990s with their daughter, Sofie. Josif was a teacher and Mila was a hairstylist, but there was war in their country, and their city was very unstable. They felt very fortunate to have a chance for a new life, and they were determined to give Sofie more opportunities. When they arrived in Chicago, they bought a small house.

Josif found work as a truck driver, and Mila stayed home and took care of Sofie. They lacked extra money for movies, meals in restaurants, and toys for their daughter. Mila wanted to find a job, but she faced many obstacles. She couldn't speak English very well, and she did not have local work experience. Sometimes, she cut her friends' hair at home. Her friends loved their new hairstyles.

Mila wanted to get a job as a professional hairstylist, but her English was a problem. Her daughter started school when she was five years old, and then Mila enrolled in English classes. Eventually, Mila found work in a hair salon. She worked ten hours every day, and her customers really liked their new hairstyles. She saved every penny to buy her own business.

Last year, Mila fulfilled her dream. The owner of the hair salon was 65 years old, and he decided to sell the salon. Now Mila has a salon of her own. "It's my passion," she says. "I love to make women more beautiful." Josif studied English and is registered in business classes at a community college. Sofie is now 20 years old, and she received a scholarship to study biology at a private university. Her dream is to become a doctor. Mila and her family are very proud of their success. They are truly models of the "American dream."

Check your answers. See page 136.

2 Answer the questions. Use the information from Exercise 1.

1. When did Mila leave her native country? *She left in the 1990s.*
2. What were Mila's and Josif's jobs before they came to the United States? ______
3. What obstacles did Mila face when she tried to find a job in the United States? ______
4. What did Mila do at home? ______
5. What did Mila buy last year? ______
6. What is Sofie's dream? ______

3 Match the sentence parts.

1. Mila and Josif left their country *f*
2. They felt fortunate ____
3. Mila had problems ____
4. She took classes ____
5. She saved her money ____
6. They are proud now ____

a. because she wanted to open her own business.
b. because she couldn't speak English well.
c. because they have fulfilled their dreams.
d. because they could start a new life.
e. because she wanted to learn English.
f. because there was a war.

4 Complete the sentences.

determined	fortunate	lacked	obstacles	passion	unstable

1. Arturo feels *fortunate* because he is taking English classes at a very good school.
2. Cooking is Karen's ______. She loves to make beautiful dinners for her family.
3. I faced many ______ when I came to this country. I couldn't speak English, and I didn't have any friends or family here.
4. My old neighborhood was very ______. There was a lot of crime, so people didn't stay there very long.
5. Boris didn't go to college in his home country because he ______ money to pay the fees.
6. I am ______ to start my own business. I am studying for a degree in business administration.

Check your answers. See page 136.

LESSON E Writing

1 Mark each sentence *S* (Success) or *O* (Obstacle).

1. He won first prize in the music contest. S
2. She got a better job with higher pay. ____
3. Her father was too sick to work. ____
4. He got a scholarship to a private university. ____
5. He didn't have enough money to go to college. ____
6. She graduated from high school. ____
7. His boss gave him a promotion at work. ____
8. She had a very bad car accident. ____

2 Read the paragraph. Then answer the questions.

My Successful Neighbor

My neighbor Mila is a successful businessperson. Her hair salon is so successful that she is planning to open a second salon next year. I'm so proud of her because when she came to this country, she did not have a job and couldn't speak English well. Mila and her hairstylists all have at least five years of experience cutting, coloring, and styling women's hair. They also study fashion magazines every month to get new ideas. Mila is living the American dream. She has proven that if you work hard and learn English, you can make your dreams come true.

1. Write one example of Mila's success.
   Mila is planning to open a second salon next year.
2. Write one fact about Mila and her employees.
   ____
3. Write another fact about Mila and her employees.
   ____
4. Write the two obstacles that Mila had when she came to America.
   ____

Check your answers. See page 136.

3 Read the information about Yasmine. Complete the outline.

Yasmine Ali's Life

Teenage years:

- *She and her family lost their home in a fire.*
- *She had to start working full-time at age 16.*
- *She couldn't finish high school because she had to work.*

Awards:

- *"Employee of the Year," Palace Hotel*
- *GED certificate, 2012*

Now:

- *She received a scholarship to study hotel management at Stone Valley Community College.*
- *She is working hard to achieve her dream of becoming a hotel manager.*

Topic sentence: *Yasmine had several obstacles on her road to success.*

Supporting details:

Obstacles: 1. ______

2. ______

3. ______

Successes: 1. ______

2. ______

3. ______

Concluding sentence: ______

4 Write a paragraph about Yasmine's obstacles and her successes. Use your outline in Exercise 3 to help you.

Yasmine had several obstacles on her road to success.

Check your answers. See page 136.

LESSON F Another view

1 Read the questions. Look at the chart. Then fill in the correct answers.

Associate's Degrees Awarded in the U.S., 2008–2009	
Field of study	**Percentage of total degrees awarded**
Business	16.2%
Computer science	3.8%
General studies	33.5%
Health professions	21.0%
Security services	4.2%
Engineering	6.7%
Other fields	14.6%

Source: National Center for Education Statistics – http://nces.ed.gov U.S. Department of Education

1. What does this chart show?
   Ⓐ the number of degrees awarded
   Ⓑ the most difficult fields of study
   ● the most popular fields of study
   Ⓓ the number of new jobs

2. What percentage of students received business degrees?
   Ⓐ 3.8%
   Ⓑ 4.2%
   Ⓒ 6.7%
   Ⓓ 16.2%

3. Security services and engineering account for what percentage of total degrees awarded?
   Ⓐ 20.0%
   Ⓑ 3.8%
   Ⓒ 10.9%
   Ⓓ 14.6%

4. Which field had the most students?
   Ⓐ Business
   Ⓑ General studies
   Ⓒ Computer science
   Ⓓ Health professions

5. Which field had the fewest students?
   Ⓐ Computer science
   Ⓑ Engineering
   Ⓒ Security services
   Ⓓ Business

6. Which statement is NOT true?
   Ⓐ More students received engineering degrees than security service degrees.
   Ⓑ More students received security services degrees than computer science degrees.
   Ⓒ More students received general studies degrees than health professional degrees.
   Ⓓ More students received business degrees than health professional degrees.

Check your answers. See page 136.

2 Write two sentences for each sign with *be supposed to* and *be not supposed to*.

stop here / keep driving

1. *You're supposed to stop here.*
2. *You're not supposed to keep driving.*

In case of fire use stairs

use the elevator / use the stairs

3. ______________________
4. ______________________

No running in pool area

walk in pool area / run in pool area

5. ______________________
6. ______________________

use this door / use the other door

7. ______________________
8. ______________________

turn left / go straight ahead

9. ______________________
10. ______________________

3 Write five true sentences about your English class with *be supposed to* or *be not supposed to*.

1. (go to sleep) *We're not supposed to go to sleep in class.*
2. (pay attention) ______________________
3. (speak English all the time) ______________________
4. (come to class on time) ______________________
5. (do our science homework in English class) ______________________

Check your answers. See page 136.

UNIT
3 Friends and family

LESSON A Listening

1 Read and answer the questions. Then listen.

TRACK 11

To: erik@cup.org
From: yjun@cup.org
Subject: I'm grounded!

Hi Erik,

I'm really sorry, but I can't go to the movies with you tomorrow. I had a big argument with my father about my grades, so now I'm grounded for a month! I'm not permitted to go anywhere after school. I have to come home and study in my room every day because he doesn't trust me to study with my friends in the library. I can't even watch TV.

My father got really angry because I got a C in history. He says I have to get an A in every class. He wants to raise me exactly the same way that he was brought up in South Korea! He doesn't understand that schools are different in the United States.

Besides, I'm interested in computers, not history. I always get As in my computer and math classes, and my counselor says I can probably get a scholarship to study computer science. I don't need an A in history to work with computers!

Can you walk home with me after school on Friday? I'd like to talk to you about my problem with my dad. It's not fair that he's so strict with me. We're not in South Korea anymore! Can you meet me on Friday? Let me know.

See you soon!
Young-jun

1. What is Young-jun's punishment?

   He is grounded for a month.

2. Why is Young-jun's father angry?

   ____

3. What are Young-jun's complaints about his father?

   ____

4. What is Young-jun interested in?

   ____

5. Why does Young-jun want to talk to Erik?

   ____

Check your answers. See page 136.

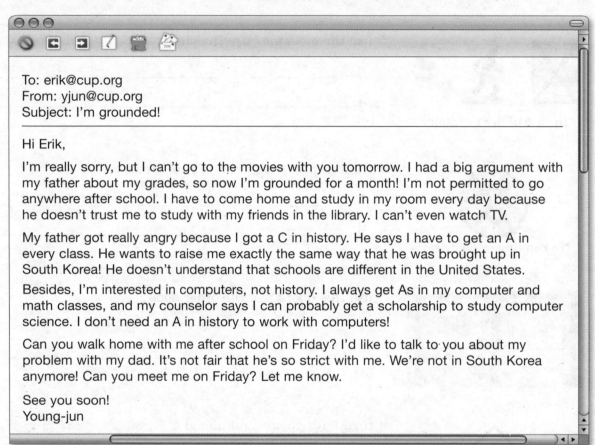

2 Circle the correct words.

1. Jason's parents permitted him to go to the party. He **could** / **couldn't** go to the party.
2. My father was very strict with me when I was a child. I had a **lot of** / **just a few** rules.
3. Adults bring up their **parents** / **children**.
4. If you trust someone, you **believe** / **don't believe** the things they say.
5. When you break the rules, you do something **bad** / **good**.

3 Complete the sentences.

break the rules	chaperone	permitted	strict
bring up	grounded	raised	trusts

1. Mrs. Alvarez is very ___strict___ with her children. They can't go out after school.
2. When I was a child, I was not ____________ to go to the store alone.
3. My father was ____________ in Iran, so his ideas about many things are different.
4. Alex is ____________ for a month because he drove his father's car without asking for permission.
5. In the past, a boy and a girl always had a ____________ when they went out together.
6. Keisha ____________ her children because they always tell her the truth.
7. Parents today ____________ their children in many different ways.
8. At school, children have to go to the principal's office if they ____________.

4 What does Mr. Burns think? Listen. Then check the correct answer.

TRACK 12

☐ Anna's mom is too strict. She should trust Anna more.

☐ Other families don't have the same problem as Anna and her mom.

☐ Anna's mom should talk to other parents with similar problems.

Check your answers. See page 136.

LESSON B Indirect questions

Study the grammar explanation on page 128.

1 Decide whether the sentences are direct or indirect. Circle the answers.

1. Where is Young-jun's father from?	(direct)	indirect
2. Do you know which class he's in?	direct	indirect
3. Can you tell me where he is now?	direct	indirect
4. What was his grade on the last history test?	direct	indirect
5. When did he talk to his counselor?	direct	indirect
6. I'd like to know what his mother thinks.	direct	indirect

2 Change the direct questions to indirect *Wh*- questions.

1. What grade is Young-jun in?

   A Do you know *what grade Young-jun is in?*

   B He's in tenth grade.

2. Where does he go to school?

   A Can you please tell me ______

   B He goes to Southwood High School.

3. Why did his father get so upset?

   A I wonder ______

   B His father is worried about Young-jun's future.

4. Where is Young-jun from?

   A Do you know ______

   B He was born in Seoul, but he was raised in this country.

5. What grades did Young-jun get in his other classes?

   A I'd like to know ______

   B He got four As and a B+.

6. What does the history teacher say about Young-jun?

   A I wonder ______

   B She says that Young-jun often looks bored in class.

Check your answers. See pages 136–137.

3 Write question mark (?) or period (.) after each sentence.

1. Do you know where they live ___?___
2. Tell me where you go to school ____
3. I wonder why he doesn't like history ____
4. I'd like to know where you went this afternoon ____
5. Can you tell me what they did ____
6. I don't know what his father's name is ____
7. Why is she grounded ____
8. How is everything at school ____

4 Read the information. Complete the conversations with indirect *Wh*- questions.

Student name: Young-jun Park	**Advisor:** Ms. Evans
ID number: 9216	**Classes:** Math 3, World History, Advanced Computer Studies, Music, English, Biology
Address: 118 Wilson Drive	

1. (can you tell me)
   A *Can you tell me what Young-jun's last name is?*
   B It's Park.
2. (do you know)
   A ________________________________
   B His address is 118 Wilson Drive.
3. (can you tell me)
   A ________________________________
   B It's 9216.
4. (I wonder)
   A ________________________________
   B He's taking six classes.
5. (I want to know)
   A ________________________________
   B Ms. Evans is his advisor.

Check your answers. See page 137.

LESSON C Indirect questions

Study the grammar explanation on page 128.

1 Complete the chart.

	Indirect question	Direct question
1.	I wonder whether Ed lives with his parents.	*Does Ed live with his parents?*
2.	Do you know if she has a job?	
3.	Can you tell me if there is a test next week?	
4.	I don't know whether Lara came to class.	
5.	I wonder if you have time to help me.	
6.	I'd like to know whether you can go to the party.	
7.	Can you tell me why your mother is so strict?	

2 Complete the conversation. Write indirect *Yes / No* questions with *if*.

1. ***A*** I haven't seen that woman before. (Can you tell me / a new student in our class)
   Can you tell me if she's a new student in our class?
   B Yes, she's new. Her name is Mimi.

2. ***A*** That's a nice name. (Do you know / from South Korea) ______
   ______
   B No, she isn't. She's from China.

3. ***A*** Really? (I'd like to know / from Beijing) ______
   B Actually, I think she's from Shanghai.

4. ***A*** (I wonder / speak English well) ______
   B Yes, she does. In fact, she speaks almost perfectly.

5. ***A*** That's interesting! (Do you know / studied English in China) ______
   ______
   B I'm not sure.

6. ***A*** (I wonder / has a job now) ______
   B I don't really know. Let's invite Mimi for a cup of coffee and ask her.
   A That's a good idea.

Check your answers. See page 137.

3 Write indirect questions. Put *if* or *whether* in the correct place.

1. (if) can you tell me we have any homework due tomorrow

   Can you tell me if we have any homework due tomorrow?

2. (whether) I wonder you can help me with my homework

3. (if) do you know the bus came

4. (whether) I'd like to know I can see the doctor today

5. (if) can you tell me Ms. Ortega is in her office now

6. (whether) do you know Svetlana lives with her parents

4 Use the words in parentheses to write indirect questions.

1. Did you get good grades in high school? (can you tell me if)

   Can you tell me if you got good grades in high school?

2. Did you have a chaperone on your dates? (I'd like to know whether)

3. Were your parents very strict with you? (I'd like to know if)

4. Were you required to come home before 10:00 p.m.? (can you tell me whether)

5. Did you argue with your parents as a teenager? (can you tell me if)

6. Did your parents like your friends in high school? (I'd like to know whether)

Check your answers. See page 137.

LESSON D Reading

1 Read and answer the questions. Then listen.

TRACK 13

BREAKING THROUGH THE BARRIERS

by Kareem Dawoud

My family immigrated to the United States when I was 10 years old because my parents wanted a better life for their family. I am the oldest of four boys in my family. When we arrived here, everything in my life changed. Suddenly, I had a new school, a new language, and new friends. English was my favorite class in school, and I got good grades. My father got a job working in a factory at night, and he learned a lot of English at work.

It was different for my mother. She stayed home to take care of me and my three brothers, so she spoke only Arabic, and she never had time to study English. Consequently, life was really difficult for her. She wanted us all to succeed in our education, but she couldn't help us. When she went shopping, I was expected to go along with her and communicate with people in the stores.

When my youngest brother started kindergarten, it created a bigger barrier to communication. Yusuf learned English very quickly, and he didn't want to speak Arabic anymore with my parents. My father laughed and called Yusuf the "little American," but my mother was very upset. Then one day, my father got information about evening English programs at my high school. My mother was really interested, but she was worried because my father worked at night. So I promised her I would take care of my brothers, and she enrolled in the program. That was two years ago. My mother is taking an advanced class now, and we're all very proud of her.

1. When did Kareem come to the U.S.? *He came to the U.S. when he was 10 years old.*
2. What happened when he moved to the U.S.? ______________________
3. Where did his father learn English? ______________________
4. Why didn't his mother learn English? ______________________
5. What did Kareem do to help his mother? ______________________
6. What is Kareem's mother doing now? ______________________

Check your answers. See page 137.

2 Complete the sentences.

barrier	create	education	hardships	success
communication	differences	generation	immigrants	

1. There are many _differences_ between life in my native country and life here.
2. Many people in my grandparents' __________ don't know how to use a computer.
3. Speaking different languages can be a __________ between parents and their children.
4. Some __________ try to keep the language and customs of their home country.
5. My parents' goal is for my sister and me to finish our __________ at a good college or university.
6. Two important factors for __________ in learning a language are practice and patience.
7. Conflicting work schedules can __________ problems in families.
8. For good __________ in families, parents should spend time talking with their children.
9. My family suffered many __________ when we first moved to this country and didn't speak the language.

3 Circle the correct words.

1. Language is one big **different** / **difference** between immigrant parents and their children.
2. Marina has a very **success** / **successful** business.
3. Many **immigrates** / **immigrants** come to this country without knowing any English.
4. Dolores can't **communication** / **communicate** with her son's friends because she doesn't speak English very well.
5. Elias is an artist. He **creates** / **creative** beautiful paintings and drawings.
6. I earned my GED certificate so that I could continue my **educated** / **education** in a four-year college.
7. My children and I have **differs** / **different** ideas about how much time they should spend studying.

Check your answers. See page 137.

LESSON E Writing

1 Read the paragraph. Then complete the outline.

Marcelo and his parents have very different ideas about ways to communicate. Marcelo likes to do everything with his computer. For example, he always sends e-mails to his friends because it's cheaper and more convenient. On birthdays and holidays, he likes to send electronic cards with music and funny cartoons from his computer. On the other hand, Marcelo's parents like to communicate in more traditional ways. They always write long letters to their relatives in their home country. On special days like birthdays, they usually make a phone call, even if it's expensive. But there's one thing they all agree about: Communicating with family and friends is very important to all of them.

Topic sentence: *Marcelo and his parents have very different ideas about ways to communicate.*

A. Marcelo: ______________________________

1. Example: ______________________________
2. Example: ______________________________

Transition: ______________________________

B. Marcelo's parents: ______________________________

1. Example: ______________________________
2. Example: ______________________________

Conclusion: ______________________________

Check your answers. See page 137.

2 Read the information about Meena and her daughter. Make an outline for a paragraph using the information.

Meena	Prita
• Prita's mother	• Meena's daughter
• likes to wear Indian clothes	• likes to wear American clothes
• favorite clothing: a sari (more traditional)	• favorite clothing: jeans and T-shirts (more comfortable)
• buys clothes in India	• buys clothes in New York

Topic sentence: *Meena and her daughter, Prita, have very different ideas about clothes.*

A. Meena: ______________________

1. Example: ______________________
2. Example: ______________________

Transition: ______________________

B. Prita: ______________________

1. Example: ______________________
2. Example: ______________________

3 Write a paragraph about the differences between Meena and Prita. Use your outline from Exercise 2.

Meena and her daughter, Prita, have very different ideas about clothes.

____

____

____

____

____

____

____

____

____

Check your answers. See page 137.

LESSON F Another view

1 Read the questions. Look at the table. Then fill in the answers.

New Permanent Residents in the U.S. by Age and Marital Status (2011)

Age	Number of residents	Marital status	Number of residents
Under 1 year	4,361	Single	405,164
1–9 years	86,845	Married	599,959
10–19 years	159,265	Divorced	26,087
20–29 years	232,272	Widowed*	26,930
30–39 years	243,772		
40–49 years	152,568		
50–59 years	95,564		
60+years	87,383		

*A widowed person is someone whose husband or wife has died.
Source: U.S. Department of Homeland Security

1. This table explains ____.
   Ⓐ where immigrants live in the U.S.
   Ⓑ the total number of married people in the U.S.
   ● the age and marital status of new permanent residents in the U.S.
   Ⓓ how to become a permanent resident of the U.S.

2. The biggest group of new permanent residents by marital status was ____.
   Ⓐ single
   Ⓑ married
   Ⓒ widowed
   Ⓓ divorced

3. The biggest group of new permanent residents by age was ____.
   Ⓐ 10–19 years old
   Ⓑ 20–29 years old
   Ⓒ 30–39 years old
   Ⓓ 40–49 years old

4. The smallest group of new permanent residents was ____.
   Ⓐ divorced
   Ⓑ widowed
   Ⓒ people over 60 years old
   Ⓓ babies less than one year old

5. There were more widowed people than ____.
   Ⓐ single people
   Ⓑ divorced people
   Ⓒ children 1–9 years old
   Ⓓ people 10–19 years old

6. Which question is *not* answered in the table?
   Ⓐ How many new residents are single?
   Ⓑ How many children are in each family?
   Ⓒ How old are the new residents?
   Ⓓ How many people over 60 years old became permanent residents?

Check your answers. See page 137.

2 Read the e-mail from Manolo to his friend Amelia in Curitiba, Brazil. Then answer the questions.

From: Manolo
To: Amelia
Subject: Hi

Hi Amelia,

I've been here in Boston for about two weeks now, and things are going pretty well. Boston reminds me of Curitiba in many ways. It's a medium-sized city with many different kinds of people.

I'm living with an American family. They're great people, but no one in the family speaks Portuguese. That means I have to practice my English! But everyone in the family likes to cook, and they're even trying some Brazilian recipes. I'm going to teach them to make my favorite cheese bread.

Going to high school here is a challenge, but the other students are very friendly. My favorite class is history because the teacher makes it very interesting. I'm going to give a presentation on Brazil next week. Wish me luck!

Best wishes from your friend,

Manolo

1. How long has Manolo been in Boston? (say) *Manolo said that he's been in Boston for two weeks.*
2. What's Boston like? (tell) *Manolo told Amelia that Boston is a medium-sized city with many different kinds of people.*
3. Who is Manolo living with? (tell) ______________________________.
4. What is Manolo going to teach them? (tell) ______________________________.
5. What are the students in the high school like? (say) ______________________________.
6. What is Manolo going to do next week? (say) ______________________________.

Check your answers. See page 137.

UNIT 4 Health

LESSON A Listening

1 Read and answer the questions. Then listen.

TRACK 14

To: jackie@cup.org
From: amy@cup.org
Subject: my job

Hi Jackie,

Thanks so much for your e-mail. I'm sorry for not writing back sooner, but I just haven't had time for anything. I started working at Bellman's Supermarket in August, and I've been working a lot of overtime hours. I'm really stressed because I have to work very quickly, and I'm afraid of making mistakes. Yesterday, I gave a customer the wrong change, and he started shouting at me. It's so hard to cope with difficult people like that!

I'm looking for a different job. I had an interview for an office job at Bellman's, and the supervisor there was really nice. The work is a lot more interesting, and it's a lot less stressful. The problem is that I still have to pass a computer test! The test covers keyboarding and two different computer programs. I love using computers, but I always feel a lot of anxiety when I take a test. I can't concentrate, and I often get a bad score.

My sister is taking a meditation class, and it's really helped her to calm down. They practice deep breathing and positive thinking. I'm going to go with her to her class tomorrow. I really hope it will help me!

Say hi to your family from me!

Love,
Amy

1. Why does Amy feel stressed at work?
   She has to work very quickly, and she's afraid of making mistakes.
2. Why does Amy want the office job?
   ____
3. What happens to Amy when she takes a test?
   ____
4. What do people do at the meditation class?
   ____

Check your answers. See page 137.

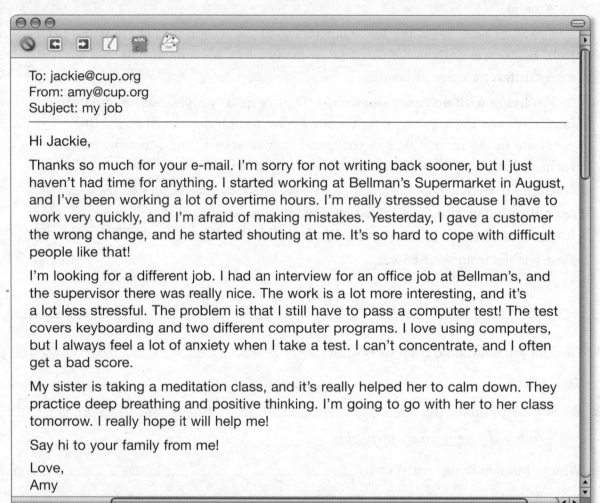

UNIT 4

2 Write the words under the correct pictures.

anxiety | calm down | concentrate | cope with stress | stressed | tense

1.

calm down

2.

3 Complete the sentences.

anxiety | calm down | cope with | stressed
breathing | concentrate | meditation | tense

A I always feel ___tense___(1) before a job interview.

B If you feel nervous, you should practice deep ________(2).

A I hope that helps. I feel so ________(3).

B It's normal to have a lot of ________(4) before an interview.

A If I don't ________(5) during the interview, I will make a lot of mistakes speaking English.

B You need to try to ________(6) before you go to the interview.

A I'm thinking about taking a ________(7) class to relax.

B Good idea! Exercising is also a good way to ________(8) stress.

4 Listen. Then check three things that helped Pete relax.

TRACK 15

- ☐ trying to practice the presentation
- ☐ taking some deep breaths
- ☐ closing his eyes
- ☐ imagining he was at the beach
- ☐ going to the beach
- ☐ trying to concentrate

Check your answers. See page 137.

LESSON **B** Modals

Study the grammar explanation on page 128.

1 Write the sentences in the correct categories.

Alan has to work on Sunday.	We don't have to take a present.
I have to take a computer test.	You don't have to answer the questions.
Naomi shouldn't spend so much money.	You should eat more vegetables.
They shouldn't worry so much.	You should look for a better job.

1. Advice

a. Naomi shouldn't spend so much money.

b. ______________________

c. ______________________

d. ______________________

2. Necessity

a. ______________________

b. ______________________

3. Lack of necessity

a. ______________________

b. ______________________

2 Complete the sentences. Use *should, shouldn't, have to,* or *don't have to.*

1. To get a driver's license, you have to take a written test first.
2. You __________ get 100 percent on the test – you only __________ get 70 percent to pass.
3. After you pass the written test, you __________ take the driving test.
4. You __________ make an appointment for the driving test too soon because you __________ practice driving a lot before the test.
5. At first, you __________ drive on busy streets because you might have an accident.
6. Later, you __________ drive to the DMV office to see the streets where you will have your driving test.
7. You __________ be tense when you take your driving test. Just relax and do your best.
8. If you don't pass the driving test the first time, you __________ feel bad. You can always try again.
9. After you pass the test, you __________ take all your friends out for a drive!

Check your answers. See page 137.

3 Complete the conversations. Use *should, shouldn't, have to,* and *don't have to.*

1. **A** We're going to a restaurant tonight.

   B That's great! We ___don't have to___ cook dinner today.

2. **A** My brother's birthday is next week.

   B You ______________ send him a card.

3. **A** Julia starts work at 5:00 a.m.

   B That's terrible. She ______________ get up at 3:30 a.m.

4. **A** There's a vocabulary test tomorrow.

   B We ______________ review all the words tonight.

5. **A** I'm really tired.

   B It's after midnight. You ______________ go to bed.

6. **A** Wow! I got 99 percent on my math test!

   B You ______________ worry so much about exams.

4 Write the opposite of each sentence. Use *should, shouldn't, have to, doesn't have to,* and *don't have to.*

1. I have to finish writing this report tonight.

   I don't have to finish writing this report tonight.

2. You should find a new place to live.

   ____

3. Wilson doesn't have to get to work early.

   ____

4. You shouldn't ask a lot of questions.

   ____

5. Risa has to meditate every day.

   ____

6. Teenagers don't have to follow their parents' advice.

   ____

Check your answers. See page 137.

LESSON C Modals

Study the grammar explanation on page 129. For a list of past participles, turn to page 134.

1 Circle the correct words.

1. My stomach hurts. I **should have** / **shouldn't have** eaten such a big dinner.
2. I hate my new apartment. I **should have** / **shouldn't have** kept my old apartment
3. I **should have** / **shouldn't have** stayed in the sun so long. Now my face is all red!
4. My phone bill is so high. I **should have** / **shouldn't have** made all those calls to Mexico last month.
5. I forgot my mother's birthday! I **should have** / **shouldn't have** written a note to myself.
6. I'm really tired today. I **should have** / **shouldn't have** gone to bed earlier last night.

2 Your friend just failed his English class. Give him advice. Use *should have* and *shouldn't have*.

1. **A** I slept during class.
   B *You shouldn't have slept during class.*
2. **A** I forgot to do my homework.
   B ______________________________
3. **A** I spoke my native language in class all the time.
   B ______________________________
4. **A** I didn't ask my teacher for help.
   B ______________________________
5. **A** I didn't go to the tutoring center.
   B ______________________________
6. **A** I left my textbook at home.
   B ______________________________
7. **A** I didn't keep a vocabulary notebook.
   B ______________________________
8. **A** I didn't practice English outside of class.
   B ______________________________

Check your answers. See page 137.

3 Look at the picture. Jessie had a job interview. Write sentences with *should have* or *shouldn't have*.

1. overslept
   She shouldn't have overslept.
2. set her alarm
   ____
3. arrive late for her interview
   ____
4. leave her house earlier
   ____
5. ask for directions to the office
   ____
6. wear jeans for her job interview
   ____
7. get more information about the job
   ____
8. forget her briefcase
   ____
9. take a pen and paper
   ____

Check your answers. See pages 137–138.

LESSON D Reading

1 Read and write the questions. Then listen.

TRACK 16

How long should I meditate?	When should I meditate?
How should I meditate?	Where is the best place to meditate?
What is meditation?	Why should I meditate?

Questions and Answers About Meditation

1. *What is meditation?*

The dictionary says that meditation is "thinking seriously about something over a period of time." It is a way to calm or relax your mind. Millions of people around the world practice meditation every day.

2. ______________________

Choose a quiet place where no one will come in. For many people, a bedroom is good.

3. ______________________

There are many different ways to meditate, but here is one that is good for beginners. Sit in a way that is comfortable for you, on the floor or in a firm chair. Loosen your clothes if they are tight. Close your eyes and relax. Now listen to the sound of your breathing. Feel the air moving in and out of your body. Concentrate on your breathing, and count each breath from one to ten. After ten breaths, start counting again from one. If your mind moves away from your breathing, don't be upset. Just notice your thoughts, and bring your mind back to your breathing. Start counting your breaths again, with "One."

4. ______________________

Some people like to meditate right after they get up in the morning before they start their daily activities. Others like to meditate in the evening before they go to bed, as a way to relax and forget about their problems.

5. ______________________

As long as you can! Start for five minutes, and try to increase the time a little bit every day. For most people, 20 minutes of meditation every day is enough to feel more relaxed. The important thing is to meditate regularly.

6. ______________________

Meditating has positive effects on both your body and your mind. Because it reduces stress, it helps prevent illness. It can make you calm in difficult situations. By practicing meditation regularly, you will be more prepared for both positive and negative changes in your life.

Check your answers. See page 138.

2 Scan the article in Exercise 1. Write the information.

1. A definition of *meditation*: thinking seriously about something over a period of time
2. An example of a good place to meditate: ____________
3. What you should concentrate on when you meditate: ____________
4. Two good times to meditate: ____________ or ____________
5. The number of minutes you should meditate to begin with: ____________
6. The number of minutes it takes to make you relaxed: ____________
7. A positive effect of meditation on your body: ____________
8. A positive effect of meditation on your mind: ____________

3 Circle the correct form of the words.

1. Tonio and Eva **meditate** / **meditation** every morning before breakfast.
2. Playing sports **regular** / **regularly** can help people to cope with stress.
3. **Ill** / **Illness** is one common example of negative stress.
4. Driving in the city is very **stress** / **stressful** for me.
5. Taking a hot bath is a good way to **loose** / **loosen** tight muscles.
6. After I practiced meditating for a few weeks, I didn't feel so **nervous** / **nervousness**.
7. Stress is the way that people **react** / **reaction** to changes in their lives.

4 Write the suffix.

ful	ion	ly	ness

1. regular ly
2. ill ____
3. depress ____
4. stress ____

Check your answers. See page 138.

LESSON E Writing

1 Circle *action* or *result*.

1. a. I take a long, hot bath.	action	result
b. My body relaxes.	action	result
2. a. I can't sleep.	action	result
b. I drink a lot of coffee.	action	result
3. a. I work for 10 hours.	action	result
b. I feel very tired.	action	result
4. a. I feel less tense.	action	result
b. I listen to quiet music.	action	result
5. a. I watch a funny movie.	action	result
b. I forget about my problems.	action	result
6. a. My muscles loosen.	action	result
b. I stretch my arms and legs.	action	result

2 Read the paragraph from Esme's journal. Complete the outline.

Monday, January 21st

I have a lot of anxiety about my job right now. When I think about all of my problems at work, I can't sleep. When I don't sleep enough, I feel tired the next day at work. If I feel tired, I can't concentrate, and then I make more mistakes. I hope that taking a meditation class will help me to cope with anxiety.

Topic sentence: *I have a lot of anxiety about my job right now.*

Action 1: ______________________

Result 1: ______________________

Action 2: ______________________

Result 2: ______________________

Action 3: ______________________

Result 3: ______________________

Check your answers. See page 138.

3 Read the information about David. Complete the outline for a journal entry.

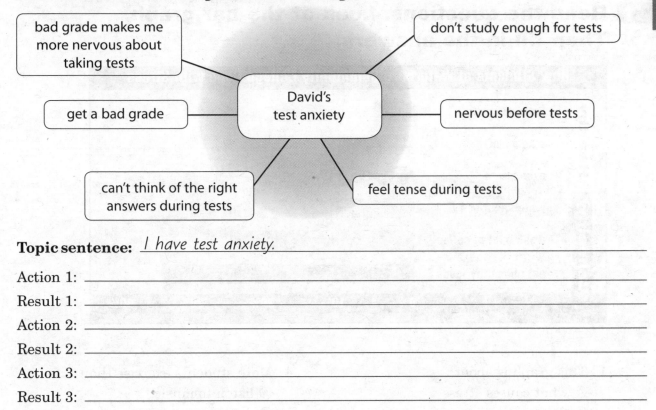

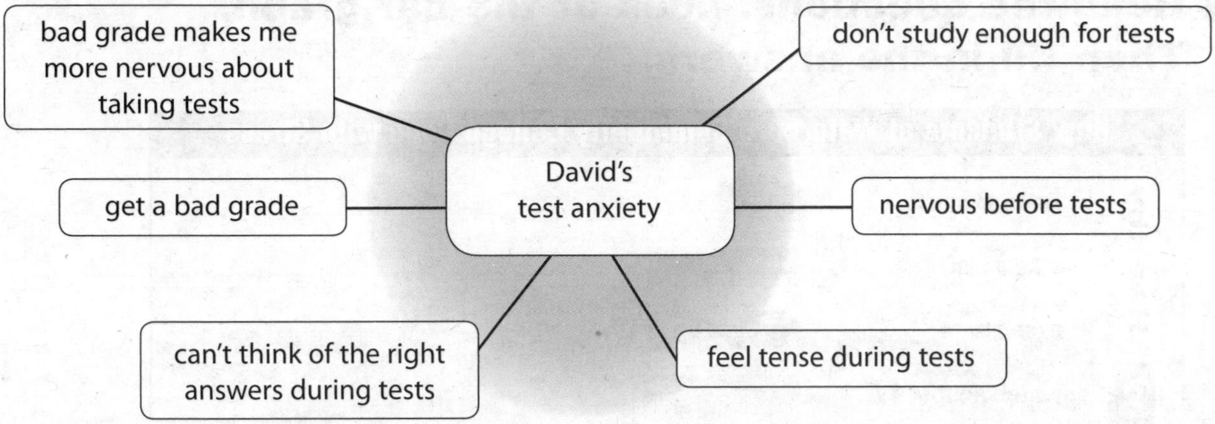

Topic sentence: *I have test anxiety.*

Action 1: ______

Result 1: ______

Action 2: ______

Result 2: ______

Action 3: ______

Result 3: ______

4 Pretend you are David. Write a paragraph in David's journal. Use your outline from Exercise 3 to help you.

I have test anxiety. ______

Check your answers. See page 138.

LESSON F Another view

1 Read the questions. Look at the bar graph. Then fill in the answers.

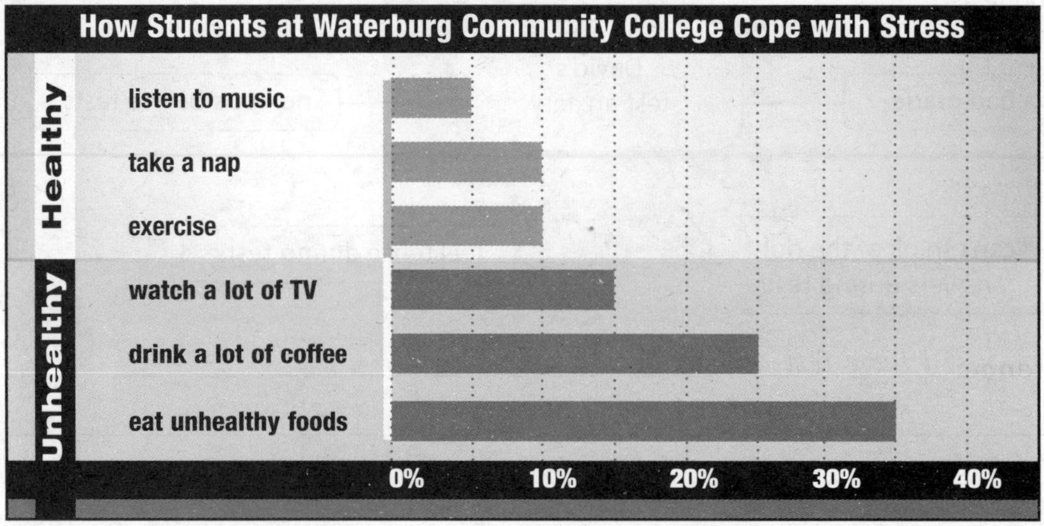

1. This graph is about ____.
   Ⓐ what causes stress
   Ⓑ the results of stress
   Ⓒ how many students suffer from stress
   ● what students do when they feel stressed

2. When students feel stressed, 25 percent of them ____.
   Ⓐ take a nap
   Ⓑ watch a lot of TV
   Ⓒ drink a lot of coffee
   Ⓓ eat unhealthy foods

3. More students watch a lot of TV than ____.
   Ⓐ exercise
   Ⓑ take a nap
   Ⓒ both a and b
   Ⓓ neither a nor b

4. More students exercise than ____.
   Ⓐ listen to music
   Ⓑ watch a lot of TV
   Ⓒ drink a lot of coffee
   Ⓓ all of the above

5. According to the graph, drinking a lot of coffee is ____.
   Ⓐ a good way to cope with stress
   Ⓑ not a healthy way to cope with stress
   Ⓒ healthier than watching a lot of TV
   Ⓓ the most popular way to cope with stress

6. According to the graph, ____ is a good way to deal with stress.
   Ⓐ taking a nap
   Ⓑ exercising
   Ⓒ both a and b
   Ⓓ neither a nor b

Check your answers. See page 138.

2 Complete the conversations with *must (not)* or *may/might (not)*.

1. **A** Paul looks terrible. Do you think he ___might___ be sick?

   B No, he isn't sick. He has a big test today, and I know he studied all night. He ___must___ be tired. He really shouldn't do that. He ___might not___ pass the test because he's too tired!

2. **A** Gina hasn't said a word to me all day. She ________ be angry with me. What do you think I did or said?

   B Maybe nothing – she ________ be angry with you at all. She ________ have some problems at home or at work. It may not have anything to do with you.

3. **A** I can't sleep at night. It's a real problem for me. Do you think the doctor ________ give me some sleeping pills?

   B Hmm. He ________ try some other things first, like asking about your habits. For example, how many cups of coffee do you drink every day?

   A Let's see. I have two in the morning, a couple at work, one after dinner and . . . .

   B Andrea, that's way too much coffee. That ________ be the reason you can't sleep. I'm almost sure of it.

4. **A** Hello, Frank? I'm calling to tell you that I ________ be able to come to dinner tomorrow. My sister's flying in from Texas, and her plane ________ be late. I'll let you know as soon as I can.

   B Don't worry about it, Rita. I know you ________ be excited to see your sister.

5. **A** Mindy ________ be very happy.

   B Why do you say that?

   A Because the Rockets lost the game last night. They're her favorite team.

   B I wouldn't be so sure. She doesn't take the games that seriously. Besides they ________ win the next game. The season isn't over yet.

Check your answers. See page 138.

UNIT
5 Around town

LESSON A Listening

1 Read and answer the questions. Then listen.

TRACK 17

My Volunteer Experience by Dani Parks

Last summer, I was a volunteer at Stone Valley Children's Hospital. I am thinking about a career in the child-care field, and I wanted to find out if I liked working with children of different ages. First, I talked to the volunteer coordinator at the hospital to get more information. Before I started, I had to attend three orientation sessions. I also had to pass some health tests. I made a commitment to volunteer two mornings a week.

Every day at the hospital was different. One of my favorite jobs was to take the toy cart to the children's rooms. They could choose toys to play with and take home, and that made their time in the hospital a lot happier. Another job I enjoyed was delivering mail and reading cards and letters to the youngest children if their parents weren't there. I also helped little children eat their lunch during mealtime. Sometimes, the volunteers did art projects like drawing and painting with the children. They really loved that!

Some people think that it's difficult to work with children who are so sick, but that isn't true. The children made me smile and laugh every time I was there. To work with sick children, you have to be patient and compassionate. You don't really need any special training – just some free time and a desire to help. I can't wait to volunteer again this summer at the hospital. I think volunteering is a worthwhile experience for everyone.

1. Write two words to describe volunteers who work with sick children.

   a. *patient*

   b. ______________

2. Write three things Dani had to do before she became a volunteer.

   a. ______________

   b. ______________

   c. ______________

3. Write four responsibilities Dani had at the hospital.

   a. ______________

   b. ______________

   c. ______________

   d. ______________

Check your answers. See page 138.

2 Circle the correct words.

1. If you can't wait to go home, you **want** / **don't want** to go home.
2. Larissa is very patient with her children. She is always **calm / angry**.
3. The residents of a building are the people who **work / live** there.
4. We had an orientation meeting before we **started / finished** volunteering.
5. I think playing sports is worthwhile for children. It's a **useless / useful** way for children to spend their time.
6. I made a commitment to the hospital. I **won't / will** volunteer one day a week.

3 Complete the sentences.

can't wait	compassionate	orientation	residents
commitment	coordinator	patient	worthwhile

1. Liz is a ___patient___ volunteer. She almost never gets upset.
2. Patrick cares about how the patients feel. He's a ______________ man.
3. Volunteering at the hospital is ______________. It helps people a lot.
4. Most of the ______________ in the nursing home are over 70 years old.
5. I ______________ to start volunteering at the animal shelter. I'm excited about it.
6. I made a ______________ to work one day every week. I volunteer every Saturday.
7. There's an ______________ meeting for the new volunteers tomorrow.
8. The volunteer ______________ will explain our duties and answer questions.

4 What does Moy have to do to volunteer at the museum? Listen. Then check two answers.

TRACK 18

- ☐ finish his degree in education
- ☐ take an orientation course
- ☐ promise to work one half day a week
- ☐ greet people who come to the museum

Check your answers. See page 138.

LESSON B Future time clauses

Study the grammar explanation on page 129.

1 Underline the future time clause in each sentence.

1. I'll help you with your homework as soon as I finish doing mine.
2. As soon as I finish cleaning the house, I'll go to the store.
3. My husband will take care of the children until I get home from work.
4. I'll volunteer every day until summer vacation ends.
5. Until my son eats all his salad, I won't give him any dessert!

2 Look at Dani's schedule. Circle the correct words.

11:00 a.m.	Arrive, check assignment, talk to nurses
11:15 a.m.	Take toys to children
12:00 noon	LUNCH
12:45 p.m.	Deliver mail, read cards to children
1:30 p.m.	Victor arrives. Art project: painting. Put paintings on walls.
3:00 p.m.	Read stories to children
4:00 p.m.	Go home

1. **A** What is the first thing that the volunteers do?

   B They check their assignment **as soon as / until** they arrive at the hospital.

2. **A** What will Dani do first?

   B She will take toys to the children **as soon as / until** it's time for lunch.

3. **A** When will she deliver the mail?

   B **As soon as / Until** the children finish their lunch, Dani will deliver the mail.

4. **A** How long will she read cards to the children?

   B She'll read cards to the children **as soon as / until** Victor arrives.

5. **A** What will she and Victor do?

   B They'll start a painting class **as soon as / until** Victor arrives.

6. **A** What will they do with the paintings?

   B **As soon as / Until** the paintings are finished, they'll put them on the walls.

Check your answers. See page 138.

3 Complete the sentences. Use *as soon as* or *until*.

1. *As soon as* Julio heard about the volunteer program for senior citizens at the hospital, he called the coordinator.
2. He can start volunteering ____________ he has finished the orientation sessions.
3. He plans to volunteer there in the afternoon ____________ the patients have dinner.
4. ____________ he starts volunteering there, the coordinator will give him a uniform.
5. He will volunteer every day ____________ school starts.

4 Write sentences about Julio's volunteer work at the hospital. Use *as soon as* or *until*.

arrived at the hospital / put on his uniform

got his assignment / went to Donnie's room

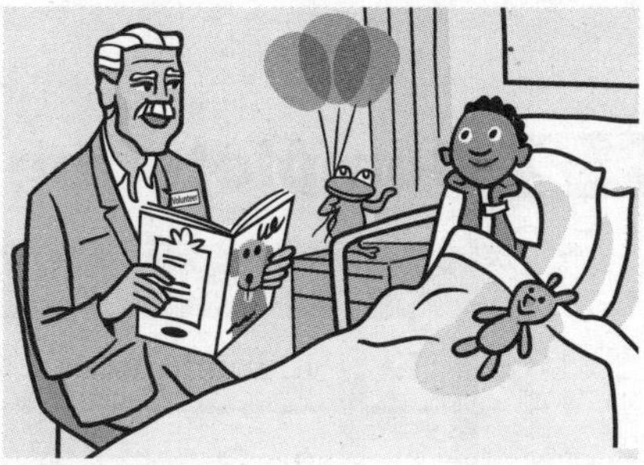
read to Donnie / was time for the doctor to come

stopped reading / doctor came in

drew pictures with Donnie / nurse brought dinner

went home / Donnie finished eating dinner

1. *As soon as Julio arrived at the hospital, he put on his uniform.*
2. ____
3. ____
4. ____
5. ____
6. ____

Check your answers. See page 138.

LESSON C Verb tense contrast

Study the grammar explanation on page 129.

1 Circle the verbs. Then write *present*, *present perfect*, or *past*.

1. I (play) games with the children in the hospital each Wednesday. present
2. Jeremy went to the homeless shelter 10 times last year. ______
3. I delivered dinners to senior citizens every Monday after school last year. ______
4. We have visited our grandfather twice so far this month. ______
5. Neena takes her grandmother to the hairdresser every week. ______
6. I have worked with elderly people many times in the past. ______

2 Complete the chart.

	Present	Past	Present perfect
1.	a. I volunteer	b. I volunteered	c. I have volunteered
2.	a.	b.	c. He has begun
3.	a.	b. They helped	c.
4.	a. I take	b.	c.
5.	a.	b.	c. We have visited
6.	a. I deliver	b.	c.

3 Write the time expressions in order, from the smallest number to the biggest number.

many times once several times twice

1. once
2. ______
3. ______
4. ______

Check your answers. See page 138.

4 Complete the conversation with the present, present perfect, or past form of the verbs.

1. **A** Please tell me a little about your volunteer work.

   B Oh, I *have volunteered* many times in my life.
   (volunteer)

2. **A** Really? Are you a volunteer now?

   B Oh, yes! Now I ____________ at the zoo twice a week.
   (volunteer)

3. **A** Have you always spent so much time at the zoo?

   B Oh, no. Last year, I ____________ in the zoo office just once a month.
   (work)

4. **A** What about this year? What's your schedule?

   B This year, I ____________ tours of the zoo several times each month.
   (give)

5. **A** Are your tours popular?

   B Yes, they are! More than a hundred people ____________ my tours so far.
   (take)

5 Look at the chart. Write sentences about the volunteers' work last month and this month.

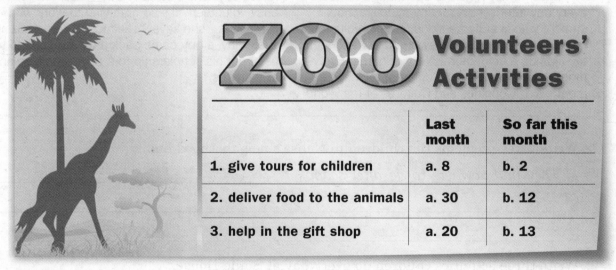

ZOO Volunteers' Activities

	Last month	So far this month
1. give tours for children	a. 8	b. 2
2. deliver food to the animals	a. 30	b. 12
3. help in the gift shop	a. 20	b. 13

1. a. *The volunteers gave tours for children eight times last month.*
   b. *The volunteers have given tours for children twice so far this month.*
2. a. ____________
   b. ____________
3. a. ____________
   b. ____________

Check your answers. See page 138.

LESSON D Reading

1 Read and answer the questions. Then listen.

TRACK 19

A Smile for Kids

When Nelisa Romero looked out the window of her living room, she saw kids – too many kids. They had nowhere to go after school. There was no park in the neighborhood, and many children were home alone without their parents.

Nelisa decided to do something about the problem. With two of her neighbors, she started Smile House in her own living room. Kids could come there as soon as school ended for the day. Smile House started with just five children. After only a few months, there were so many kids that Nelisa had to look for more volunteers and later rent a bigger building.

Today, Smile House is open for three hours every day after school for any middle school student who is at home alone. Twenty volunteers help the kids during "homework hour," and then the kids do a computer activity or game. Every month, they learn about a different topic. This month, it's "Countries and Cultures of the World."

For Nelisa, helping these children is very rewarding. "Many of them feel insecure because they don't understand their classes in school," she says. One of the children is visually impaired, and other kids have grave family problems. But at Smile House, they all have fun learning together. Smile House is different from school. They don't have to participate in any activity if they're not interested.

In the last ten years, more than a thousand children have participated in the programs at Smile House, and today businesses donate a lot of money to support the organization. But Nelisa says she's still just a volunteer – a very busy volunteer! "It's so gratifying to work with these kids," she says. "Their tenacity is amazing! Yesterday, a boy came back after six years to tell us about his scholarship to a private college and to thank us."

1. Write three problems the children in Nelisa's neighborhood had.
   a. *They had nowhere to go after school.*
   b. ______________________
   c. ______________________
2. Write three activities children do every day at Smile House.
   a. ______________________
   b. ______________________
   c. ______________________
3. How is Smile House different from school?

____

Check your answers. See page 138.

2 Number the events in the correct order. Use the information from Exercise 1.

____ Someone came back to say thank you to Nelisa.
____ Smile House was in Nelisa's living room.
____ Nelisa looked for more volunteers.
__1__ Nelisa saw children playing in the street.
____ Smile House moved to a bigger building.
____ Nelisa decided to start an after-school program for children.

3 Circle the correct words.

1. Freedom means you **are** / **aren't** allowed to do the things you want to do.
2. A grave illness is **very serious / not serious**.
3. My volunteer work is so rewarding! I really **enjoy / don't like** it.
4. If your vision is impaired, you **can / can't** see well.
5. Isabel is insecure about her grades. She feels **happy / worried** about school.
6. Malik has so much tenacity! He always **tries hard / stops trying**.
7. For me, learning English is very gratifying. I'm very **proud / sad** that I have learned so much already.

4 Complete the sentences.

freedom	grave	insecure	tenacity
gratifying	impaired	rewarding	

1. Volunteering at the children's hospital is very __rewarding__ for me because I help the children.
2. I help my grandmother go for walks around the neighborhood because she feels ____________ about walking alone.
3. Miguel's hearing is ____________. He can't hear very well.
4. If you have ____________, you keep trying even when something is very difficult.
5. Some patients have to stay in the hospital for many weeks because they have a ____________ illness.
6. Seeing the results of your volunteer work is very ____________.
7. Retired people have the ____________ to spend a lot of time volunteering.

Check your answers. See page 138.

LESSON E Writing

1 Read the paragraph. Then answer the questions.

Tony is one of the kindest people I know. He has always loved music and singing. When he was 16, his grandfather had to move to a nursing home. Tony's grandfather felt bored there, and Tony went to visit him as often as possible. One day, Tony brought his guitar with him to the nursing home and played some old songs for his grandfather. Some of the other residents came to listen, and they all had big smiles on their faces. Tony wanted to do something for the residents in the nursing home. Every Saturday while he was in high school, Tony went to the nursing home to play his guitar. He taught the residents songs so that they could all sing together. Tony made a great difference in the lives of these elderly people. He made their days happier with his music. Now he goes to college in another city, but he still volunteers at nursing homes. He wants to become a social worker for elderly people.

1. Who made a difference? *Tony made a difference.*
2. What did he do? ______
3. Why did he do it? ______
4. Where did he do it? ______
5. When did he do it? ______
6. How did he make a difference? ______

Check your answers. See page 138.

2 Look at the diagram. Complete the chart.

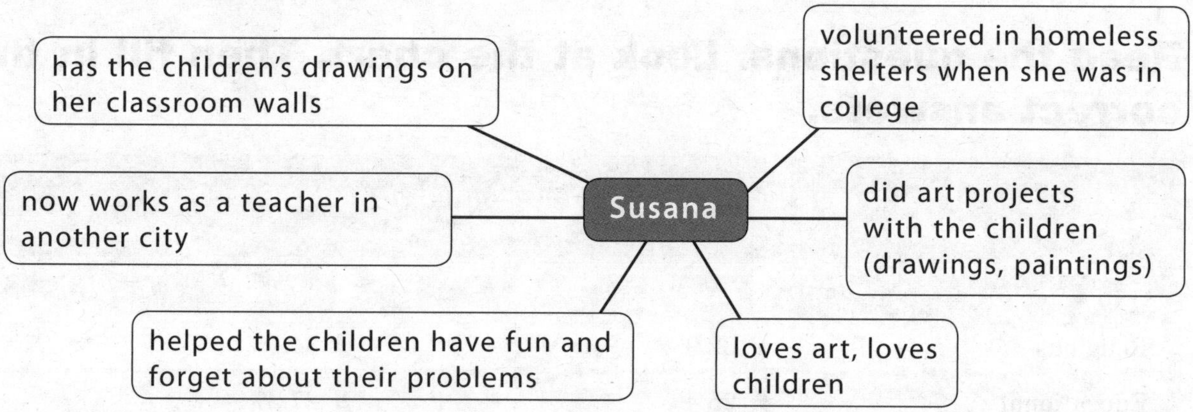

1. **Who** made a difference?	*Susana*
2. **What** did she do with the children?	
3. **When** did she do it?	
4. **Where** did she do it?	
5. **Why** did she do it?	
6. **How** did she make a difference?	
7. **What** does she do now?	

3 Write a paragraph about Susana. Use your chart from Exercise 2 to help you.

Susana has made a difference in the lives of many children.

Check your answers. See page 138.

LESSON F Another view

1 Read the questions. Look at the chart. Then fill in the correct answers.

Main Types of Volunteer Work for Men and Women in the U.S., 2010
Percentages by Type

Type of work	Men	Women
Religious	32.9%	34.5%
Educational	25.4%	27.2%
Community service	13.6%	13.1%
Civic and professional	6.4%	4.5%
Hospital and other health	6.5%	9.0%
Sports and arts	3.9%	2.8%
Public safety	2.2%	0.6%
Environment	2.4%	2.5%
Other	4.0%	3.5%

Source: Bureau of Labor Statistics, 2010

1. What question does the chart answer?
   Ⓐ How many hours do volunteers work in the U.S.?
   ● What kinds of volunteer work do men and women do?
   Ⓒ How many volunteer workers are there in the U.S.?
   Ⓓ Where are volunteers most needed in the U.S.?

2. Women do more volunteer work than men in the area of ____.
   Ⓐ hospitals and other health
   Ⓑ public safety
   Ⓒ sports and arts
   Ⓓ community service

3. Men do more volunteer work than women in the area of ____.
   Ⓐ hospitals and other health
   Ⓑ education
   Ⓒ religious groups
   Ⓓ community service

4. The smallest percentage of women volunteers work in ____.
   Ⓐ public safety organizations
   Ⓑ sports and arts groups
   Ⓒ environmental groups
   Ⓓ civic and professional groups

5. The most popular type of volunteer work for men and women is ____.
   Ⓐ public safety
   Ⓑ religious
   Ⓒ educational
   Ⓓ community service

6. The percentage is almost the same for men and women who volunteer in ____.
   Ⓐ hospital and other health organizations
   Ⓑ civic and professional groups
   Ⓒ environmental groups
   Ⓓ public safety organizations

Check your answers. See page 139.

2 Complete the sentences with affirmative or negative forms of *used to* and *be used to*.

1. Elena ___*used to go*___ (go) to Puerto Rico for her vacation every year. For the last two years she's gone to Alaska, but she doesn't like it. She says, "I' ___*m not used to traveling*___ (travel) in a such a cold place. I prefer the warm weather."
2. I ______________ (like) getting up early, but now I ______________ (get up) at 5:00 a.m. and I actually enjoy the morning.
3. Now Ariana ______________ (speak) in public, but it ______________ (make) her very nervous.
4. When Marta first moved to her own apartment, she ______________ (get) very lonely. Now she ______________ (live) alone. In fact, she likes it.
5. We ______________ (own) a car. We didn't need one. Now we have one, but we ______________ (drive) it.
6. When Alex lived at home, his mother ______________ (clean) his room for him. Now he has his own house and it's a mess! He ______________ (do) his own cleaning.

3 Write true sentences about yourself. Use the affirmative or negative of *be used to*.

1. (stay up late)
   I'm used to staying up late. or *I'm not used to staying up late.*
2. (get up early every day)
   ____
3. (speak English all the time)
   ____

Check your answers. See page 139.

UNIT 6 Time

LESSON A Listening

1 Complete the story. Then listen.

TRACK 20

convenient	distracting	innovative	spam
devices	electronic	manual	text message

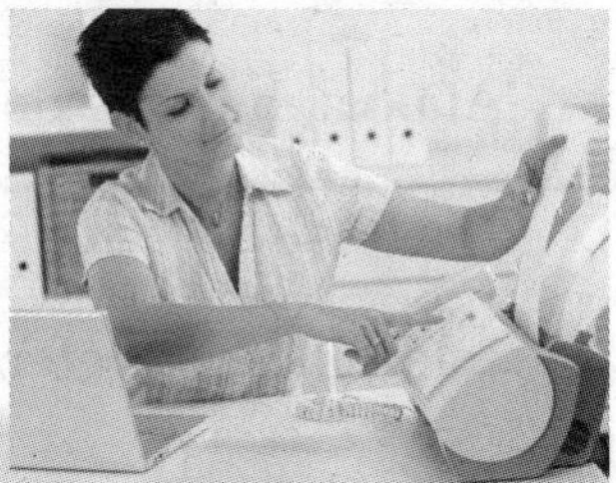

I work in an office, and my job has changed a lot in the last few years. In that time, we have gotten a lot of innovative (1) technology in our company. Some of these time-saving ____________ (2) work really well and are very ____________ (3). For example, I love my cell phone. People can reach me when I'm outside of the office, and they can also send me a quick ____________ (4). I also really like my ____________ (5) postal scale. It gives me the correct weight of letters and packages so I can print my own mailing labels. That means I never have to go to the post office. It's much better than my old ____________ (6) scale.

Other technology doesn't really save any time at all. E-mail is one example. Although it's very fast, it can also be very ____________ (7). Often I get messages when I'm working on something else, and then I forget what I was doing. Another problem is that so many messages are just ____________ (8). I think the worst device, though, is my laptop computer. In the past, I had to finish all my work before Friday evening. Now, my boss expects me to take my computer home and work on the weekend. That doesn't save me any time at all!

2 Circle *T* (True) or *F* (False).

1. The writer works in a library.	T	(F)
2. The writer likes all new technology.	T	F
3. The writer has an electronic scale now.	T	F
4. The writer thinks that e-mail doesn't save any time.	T	F
5. The writer likes laptop computers.	T	F
6. The writer uses a laptop computer to work at home.	T	F

Check your answers. See page 139.

3 Circle the correct words.

1. A device is a **machine** / **person** that does a special job.
2. Catherine felt very **happy / upset** when she found 27 spam messages in her in-box today.
3. If something is convenient, it makes your life **easier / harder**.
4. Mike **read / listened to** a text message from his wife.
5. If something is manual, you use **electricity / your hands** to operate it.
6. I'm trying to answer my e-mail, but that TV program is distracting me. Could you please turn it **on / off**?
7. It's an electronic calculator. It works with a small **computer / light** inside it.
8. An innovative product is made with **old / new** technology.

4 Complete the sentences.

convenient	distracting	innovative	spam
devices	electronic	manual	text message

1. I've never seen a computer program like this one. It's very ___innovative___.
2. My in-box is full of advertising messages I didn't ask for. I really hate ____________!
3. You shouldn't talk on your cell phone while you drive. It's too ____________.
4. Some photographers prefer ____________ cameras because they want to change settings by hand.
5. Please send Jim a ____________. Tell him we're going to be a little late.
6. Some ____________ games use a lot of batteries. That can be expensive.
7. The microwave oven is one of the greatest time-saving ____________.
8. The camera on my cell phone is very ____________. I can take pictures anytime.

5 Listen. Then check two true statements.

TRACK 21

- [ ] Hank says he doesn't want to spend time commuting.
- [ ] Hank wants to invent a new computer game.
- [ ] With Hank's teleport machine, people will travel very quickly.
- [ ] Hank doesn't think that our lives are too fast.

Check your answers. See page 139.

LESSON B Clauses of concession

Study the grammar explanation on page 130.

1 Match the sentence parts. Then write the sentences.

1. Although sending e-mail is fast, _d_
2. Even though I have a cell phone, ____
3. Although I sometimes use a microwave, ____
4. Even though I have a driver's license, ____
5. Although digital cameras are innovative, ____
6. Even though I don't have air-conditioning, ____

a. I don't own a car.
b. I prefer old cameras.
c. I don't make many calls with it.
d. I think sending a letter is friendlier.
e. I think the food doesn't taste good.
f. the temperature in my house is comfortable.

1. _Although sending e-mail is fast, I think sending a letter is friendlier._
2. ____________________
3. ____________________
4. ____________________
5. ____________________
6. ____________________

2 Read the survey. Write sentences about what David prefers with *although* or *even though*.

Name: *David King* ✗ = sometimes ✓ = usually

	✗ = sometimes		✓ = usually	
1. How do you write to friends?	✗	e-mails	✓	letters
2. How do you wash your dishes?	✓	by hand	✗	dishwasher
3. How do you get the news?	✗	TV	✓	radio
4. What do you use when it's hot?	✗	air conditioner	✓	fan
5. How do you go to work?	✓	bicycle	✗	car

1. _Although David sometimes writes e-mails, he prefers to write letters._ (although)
2. ____________________ (even though)
3. ____________________ (although)
4. ____________________ (even though)
5. ____________________ (although)

Check your answers. See page 139.

3 Combine the sentences. Use the words in parentheses.

1. Nora has a new cell phone. She likes her old cell phone better. (even though)
   Even though Nora has a new cell phone, she likes her old cell phone better.
2. I used my GPS. I still couldn't find the way to your house. (although)
3. Omar works in an office. He doesn't like to use computers. (although)
4. I sent you three text messages. You never wrote back. (even though)
5. My mother bought a digital camera. She doesn't know how to take pictures with it. (although)
6. Mr. Cho gets a lot of spam. He likes using e-mail. (even though)
7. I have a dishwasher. I prefer to wash the dishes by hand. (although)

4 Rewrite the sentences. Put the second part of the sentence first.

1. I usually cook on the stove even though I have a microwave.
   Even though I have a microwave, I usually cook on the stove.
2. Although I put in new batteries, my camera doesn't work.
3. He refuses to get a new car although his old car often breaks down.
4. Even though the store was having a sale, the clothes were too expensive.
5. I prefer to travel by train even though a plane is faster.
6. Although a fan is cheaper, I prefer to use the air conditioner.
7. I still write e-mails even though most people now prefer text messages.

Check your answers. See page 139.

LESSON C Clauses of reason and concession

Study the grammar explanation on page 130.

1 Circle the correct answers.

1. Because laptop computers are more expensive than desktop computers,
   a. I bought a laptop.
   (b.) I bought a desktop.
2 Although Mrs. Greer has a phone book,
   a. she uses her phone book.
   b. she calls directory assistance.
3. Because shopping online is more convenient than shopping in stores,
   a. I always shop online.
   b. I always shop in stores.
4. Although Jessica doesn't really like modern technology,
   a. she has a cell phone.
   b. she doesn't have a cell phone.
5. Because Dan doesn't have much time,
   a. he never cooks in a microwave.
   b. he usually cooks in a microwave.
6. Although I asked a lot of questions about my new cell phone,
   a. I understand how to use it.
   b. I don't understand how to use it.
7. Because my new car has a GPS system in it,
   a. I usually get lost.
   b. I never get lost anymore.

2 Complete the sentences. Use *although* or *because*.

1. ___*Although*___ I have a big family, we have only one TV in our house.
2. My father bought a digital camera ____________ he never used one before.
3. Carlos uses a laptop computer ____________ he travels a lot for his job.
4. I dry my clothes outside on the line ____________ it takes a long time.
5. ____________ Alicia wants to save money, she takes the bus to work.
6. We put central air-conditioning in our house ____________ the weather is very hot in this part of the country.

Check your answers. See page 139.

3 Lisa and her friend Linda do everything differently. Compare them. Use *because* and *although*.

1. Lisa: bake cakes (fun)

   Linda: buy cakes (faster)

   Lisa bakes cakes because it's fun. Although baking cakes is more fun,

   Linda buys cakes because it's faster.

2. Lisa: use a cell phone (convenient)

   Linda: use a regular phone (cheaper)

   ____

   ____

3. Lisa: cook in a microwave (fast)

   Linda: cook in a regular oven (makes food taste better)

   ____

   ____

4. Lisa: read news online (quick)

   Linda: read the newspaper (relaxing)

   ____

   ____

5. Lisa: travel by plane (comfortable)

   Linda: travel by train (interesting)

   ____

   ____

6. Lisa: take lunch to work (less expensive)

   Linda: buy lunch (easier)

   ____

   ____

Check your answers. See page 139.

LESSON D Reading

1 Read and number the steps in the correct order. Then listen.

TRACK 22

To: misha@cup.org
From: jaesun@cup.org
Subject: your phone problem

Hi Misha,

I think I found an answer for your phone problem! You said you had outrageous phone bills because of your calls to your friends in your native country. Do you know about Internet telephoning? I just tried it, and it's amazing! Instead of a phone, you use your computer to make phone calls through the Internet. Best of all, it's free!

My brother showed me how it works. First, you go to a special Web site and sign up. I got a user name and a password. Your friend has to sign up, too. Then you need headphones to listen to the call and a microphone to speak into. Luckily, I already had both of those. To make a call, you type in your friend's user name. Your friend sees a special symbol on his computer screen, and then you can start talking. You can talk as long as you want! At the end of the call, you just close the Web site.

Last night, I talked to my cousin in Seoul for more than an hour, and it didn't cost anything! I had so much fun! Next week, it's my aunt's birthday, so I'm going to call her. I'll talk to all my relatives there, and we can have a virtual birthday party.

You should try it, too. The cost is very reasonable – you can buy a microphone and headphones for $20, and after that, all your calls are free. My brother says that Internet telephoning is very popular in a lot of countries now. If you want, I'll come over to your house to help you with it.

See you in class!
Jae-sun

____ Talk to your friend.

____ Get headphones and a microphone.

__1__ Go to an Internet telephoning Web site.

____ Close the Web site.

____ Get a user name and password.

____ Type your friend's user name.

Check your answers. See page 139.

2 Write *F* for fact or *O* for opinion. Use the information from Exercise 1.

1. Misha's phone bills are outrageous. __O__
2. You use your computer to make calls over the Internet. ____
3. Internet telephoning is amazing. ____
4. You need headphones to listen to the call. ____
5. The cost of a microphone and headphones is very reasonable. ____
6. A microphone and headphones cost $20. ____
7. You have to create a user name and password. ____
8. It is easy to call people on the Internet. ____

3 Circle the correct words.

1. My phone bill last month was so high because I made **a lot of / just a few** calls.
2. I think videoconferencing is amazing. I really **enjoy / don't like** it.
3. The price of this laptop computer is very reasonable. It's **expensive / not expensive**.
4. Jennie was in a car accident a few months ago. Luckily, she **was / wasn't** hurt.
5. If something is popular, **many / only a few** people like it.
6. A virtual meeting happens **online / in a room**.

4 Complete the sentences.

amazing	luckily	outrageous	popular	reasonable	virtual

1. My new computer is ____amazing____. It's so small, and it weighs just a few pounds!
2. Camera phones are very ________________ now. All of my friends have them.
3. We had a surprise quiz in class. ________________, I studied a lot the night before, so I was ready for it.
4. I think the price of gasoline now is ________________. It's getting more expensive every day!
5. Pilar went to a videoconferencing center and had a ________________ party with all of her relatives in Spain.
6. Cell phones used to be very expensive, but they are much more ________________ now. You can get a good one for a low price.

Check your answers. See page 139.

LESSON E Writing

1 Read the paragraph. Then complete the diagrams.

A Device That Doesn't Save Time

For me, a cell phone has some advantages, but it has more disadvantages. Although I have a cell phone, it doesn't really save me very much time. It is very convenient because I can make calls wherever I am. I can use it to take pictures, and it's also very good in an emergency. But my mother sometimes calls and talks for an hour when I'm busy. I often forget my cell phone at home, so I have to go back to get it. It's easy to lose my phone, and then I spend a lot of time looking all over my house to find it. And I always have to be careful not to break it.

Two months ago, I bought a new cell phone. Even though I read the instructions many times, I couldn't understand how to use it. I had to go back to the store and ask the salesperson. I guess another disadvantage is the time it takes to learn how to use it.

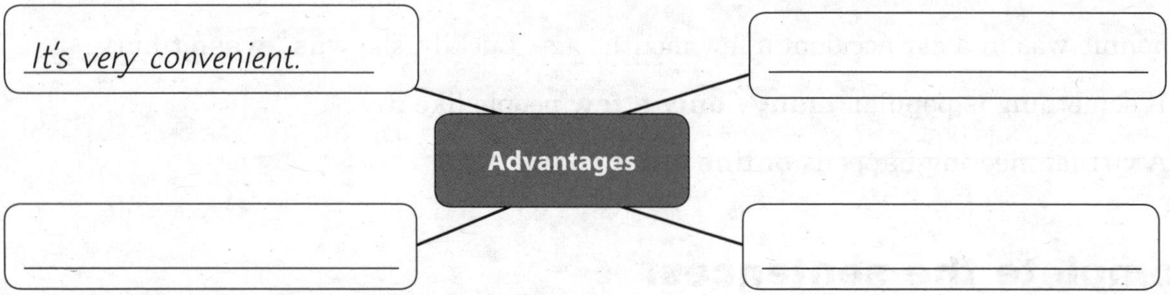

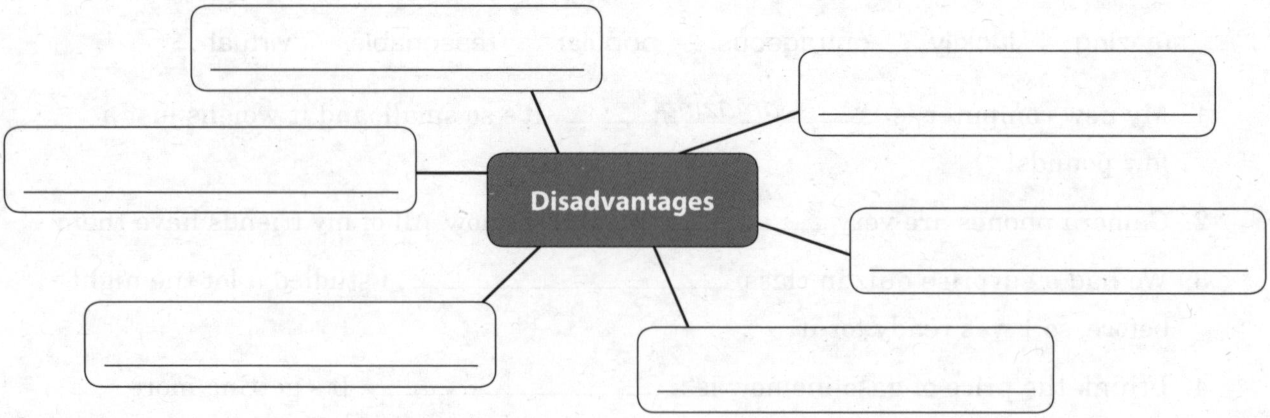

Check your answers. See page 139.

2 Read the sentences. Then complete the chart.

- You can find a lot of information on the Internet.
- You can write e-mails or reports easily.
- They cost a lot of money.
- You can learn useful skills for your job.
- You can play amazing games.
- Computer games make it easy to waste time.
- You have to spend a lot of time learning to use them.

Advantages of home computers	Disadvantages of home computers
1. *You can find a lot of information on the Internet.*	1.
2.	2.
3.	3.
4.	

3 Write a paragraph about home computers. Use your chart from Exercise 2 to help you.

There are advantages and disadvantages of having a home computer.

Check your answers. See page 139.

LESSON F Another view

1 Read the questions. Look at the table. Then fill in the answers.

Reader survey: Who owns electronic products?

Which electronic products do you own?	Percent of readers: Ages 18–29	Percent of readers: Ages 30 and over
Cell phone	92%	67%
Digital camera	93%	62%
DVD player	95%	82%
Laptop computer	90%	60%
Television	96%	98%

1. Which question does this table answer?
   Ⓐ How much do electronic products cost?
   ● Which electronic products are the most popular?
   Ⓒ What are the newest electronic products?
   Ⓓ Why do people buy electronic products?

2. How many groups of people does this table talk about?
   Ⓐ two
   Ⓑ three
   Ⓒ four
   Ⓓ five

3. What product do 82 percent of readers ages 30 and over own?
   Ⓐ a cell phone
   Ⓑ a DVD player
   Ⓒ a digital camera
   Ⓓ a laptop computer

4. What was the most popular product for both groups of people?
   Ⓐ a cell phone
   Ⓑ a television
   Ⓒ a digital camera
   Ⓓ a laptop computer

5. Which product was more popular with older people than younger people?
   Ⓐ a television
   Ⓑ a cell phone
   Ⓒ a DVD player
   Ⓓ a laptop computer

6. Which statement is true?
   Ⓐ More older people have digital cameras.
   Ⓑ Cell phones are the most popular products for younger people.
   Ⓒ More younger people have laptop computers.
   Ⓓ DVD players are the most popular products for older people.

Check your answers. See page 139.

2 Complete the sentences with *so* or *such*.

1. ATMs are ___so___ convenient that banks don't have to hire as many employees.
2. E-mail is ____________ a convenient way to communicate that people no longer write letters.
3. Computer games are ____________ interesting that many people can't stop playing them.
4. Internet news services have become ____________ popular that many print newspapers are going out of business.
5. The music I downloaded has ____________ poor sound quality that I don't enjoy listening to it.
6. It's now ____________ easy to download movies to your TV that many video stores have closed.
7. My new computer has ____________ a large screen that it doesn't fit on my desk.
8. Cell phones have become ____________ a serious problem in the classroom that many schools don't allow students to bring them to school.

3 Put the words in order to make sentences.

1. so / upload photos / is / my Internet connection / I can't / slow that
   My Internet connection is so slow that I can't upload photos.
2. an old cell phone / I can't / I have such / send text messages / that
   ____.
3. a great photographer / easy to use / digital cameras / that anyone can be / are so
   ____.
4. expensive that / to buy them / many new TVs are / so / most people can't afford
   ____.
5. such / that no one in the office / that's / can understand it / a difficult computer program
   ____.

Check your answers. See page 139.

UNIT **7** Shopping

LESSON **A** Listening

1 Read and answer the questions. Then listen.

TRACK 23

To: mateo@cup.org
From: hassan@cup.org
Subject: problem with my DVD player

Hi Mateo,

I'm really sorry, but we can't watch DVDs at my house tonight. I had to take my new DVD player back to Electronics World. There was a big sale, and I got a great price on it. But when I brought it home, it was too difficult to use. Even though I read the instruction book three times, I couldn't understand how it worked. My brother tried, too.

It was a BIG problem returning it to the store. I bought it two weeks ago, and I couldn't find the receipt. I looked everywhere. Finally, I found it in my desk. I went back to Electronics World yesterday, and I had to wait in a long line for customer service. The clerk wasn't very helpful. Even though the DVD player was in perfect condition, he said customers can only get a refund if the merchandise is defective. I had the box and the warranty card, but he didn't want to give me a refund. Finally, he agreed to give me a store credit. But I was really upset by then, so I didn't want to choose another DVD player. I just went home.

Next time, I'll be more careful. I know that I should always ask about the store policy for refunds and exchanges before I buy anything!

Let's go out and see a movie tonight, OK?

See you later,
Hassan

1. What did Hassan buy? *He bought a new DVD player.*
2. What was the problem with it? ______
3. When did he buy it? ______
4. What is the store's policy for refunds? ______
5. What did the clerk give Hassan? ______
6. What did Hassan learn? ______

Check your answers. See page 139.

2 Circle the answers.

1. Ben works in customer service. He helps people who want to **look at / return** merchandise.
2. This cell phone is defective. It is **broken / not the right size**.
3. If you exchange a sweater you bought, you get **a different sweater / your money back**.
4. That camera has a warranty. If it's defective, you can get **a new camera / store credit**.
5. You can use a store credit to buy things at **the same / a different** store.
6. The store gave me a refund because the CD didn't play. The store gave me **a new CD / my money back**.

3 Complete the sentences.

condition	defective	merchandise	store credit
customer service	exchange	refund	warranty

1. If you order something by mail and it doesn't work, you can ____exchange____ it.
2. My new CD player is ____________. It won't play my CDs.
3. This computer has a three-year ____________. If there's a problem, the company will fix it.
4. Take the jacket to the ____________ department. You can return it there.
5. Many customers don't want a store credit. They prefer a ____________.
6. This dress looks new. It's in perfect ____________.
7. There's a big sale at Sam's Music Store – 20 percent off all ____________.
8. The store didn't give me my money back. I got a ____________.

4 Listen. Then check one true statement.

TRACK 24

- ☐ The customer dropped the microwave and broke it.
- ☐ The customer has the box but not the receipt.
- ☐ The customer wants to see the store manager.
- ☐ The customer paid the return charge.

Check your answers. See page 139.

LESSON B Subject-pattern adjective clauses

Study the grammar explanation on page 130.

1 Underline the adjective clauses with *that* or *who*.

1. Anita wants to get a camera that has a big screen.
2. I went to a big store that sells all kinds of computers.
3. The clerk who helped us was Mr. Tranh.
4. A camera that takes good pictures is sometimes expensive.
5. Many people who buy a new cell phone don't know how to use it.
6. I thanked my friend who told me about that store.
7. The woman who works in customer service is Ms. Watkins.
8. The computers that are in our computer lab are very old.

2 Match the sentence parts. Then write the sentences.

1. I have a friend _d_
2. I prefer cell phones ____
3. I bought a digital camera ____
4. There are some students in my class ____
5. Maria likes to shop in stores ____
6. I know a Web site ____
7. He loves restaurants ____

a. that have good customer service.
b. that has great prices on video cameras.
c. that fits in my pocket.
d. who knows a lot about computers.
e. that serve Mexican food.
f. who always shop online.
g. that have large screens.

1. I have a friend who knows a lot about computers.
2. ______________________________
3. ______________________________
4. ______________________________
5. ______________________________
6. ______________________________
7. ______________________________

Check your answers. See page 140.

3 Circle the correct words. In some sentences, both words are correct.

1. The person **who** / **that** told me about this store is my neighbor.
2. Erin has a cell phone **who** / **that** takes great pictures.
3. Can you show me a camera **who** / **that** is easy to use?
4. Most people want to shop in stores **who** / **that** have low prices.
5. I have a brother **who** / **that** works in a computer store.
6. Some people **who** / **that** have cell phones never use them.
7. I need a video camera **who** / **that** can fit in my hand.
8. The clerk **who** / **that** works in customer service gave me a discount.

4 Combine the sentences. Change the second sentence into an adjective clause with *that* or *who*.

1. I wanted to get a microwave. It can cook big dinners.
   I wanted to get a microwave that can cook big dinners.
2. I had a microwave. It was too small.
   ____
3. I went to a department store. It was having a big sale.
   ____
4. The clerk didn't know anything about microwaves. She tried to help me.
   ____
5. She sold me a microwave. It can cook a whole chicken.
   ____
6. The microwave didn't fit in my kitchen. It was on sale.
   ____
7. Another clerk said that I needed my receipt to return the microwave. He talked to me.
   ____
8. I couldn't find the receipt. It showed the price of the microwave.
   ____
9. I will never shop again at the store! The store sold me that microwave.
   ____

Check your answers. See page 140.

LESSON C Object-pattern adjective clauses

Study the grammar explanation on page 130.

1 Zayna loves to go shopping for clothes. Write sentences about her clothes. Use adjective clauses with *that*.

1. jewelry / found at a garage sale / very cheap
   The jewelry that she found at a garage sale was very cheap.
2. jeans / bought online / not expensive
   ____
3. jacket / bought at a secondhand store / only $20
   ____
4. shoes / got at a department store / on sale
   ____
5. blouse / ordered from a catalog / the wrong color
   ____
6. dress / purchased on the Internet / 50 percent off
   ____

2 Complete the sentences. Use an adjective clause with *that*.

1. (I bought a used car) The *used car that I bought* looks very new.
2. (we talked to a salesperson) The ______________ explained the different kinds of cell phones.
3. (Justin wants a computer) The ______________ is good for playing games.
4. (my parents gave me a camera) I'm using the ______________.
5. (you told me about the store) Yesterday, I went to ______________.
6. (I ordered pants online) The ______________ were too small.
7. (she received a birthday present) The ______________ was defective.
8. (I want the rug) The ______________ is from the catalog.
9. (she likes the coffee table) The ______________ is on sale.

Check your answers. See page 140.

3 Michelle had bad luck shopping yesterday. Write sentences about what she bought. Use an adjective clause with *that*.

1. The shoes are the wrong size. (bought on sale)
   The shoes that she bought on sale are the wrong size.
2. The lamp is broken. (ordered on the Internet)
3. The CD is scratched. (found at a secondhand store)
4. The cell phone is damaged. (got yesterday)
5. The meat is spoiled. (picked up from the supermarket)

4 Combine the sentences. Change the second sentence into an adjective clause with *that*.

1. Alan is a student. I met him in my English class.
   Alan is a student that I met in my English class.
2. The old computer suddenly stopped working. He always used it for his homework.
3. The report is due in three days. Alan is writing a report.
4. The repair shop couldn't fix his computer. He went to a repair shop.
5. He asked for advice from a neighbor. He knows his neighbor very well.
6. His neighbor has some old computers. He repaired the computers.
7. Alan bought a computer for only $100. His neighbor didn't need the computer.

Check your answers. See page 140.

LESSON D Reading

1 Read and complete the sentences. Then listen.

TRACK 25

Beth Weber
96 Market Street
Galveston, TX 77553
June 12, 2013

To Whom It May Concern:

I am writing about a problem that I had with a purchase from your company.

Last month, I went to your jewelry store to buy a birthday present for my mother. The salesperson showed me a beautiful ring that was on sale. However, my mother has very small hands, and the store didn't have that ring in her size. The clerk said that your Web site had the same ring in more sizes. So I went online and bought the ring that I liked in my mother's size.

After I received the ring, I looked at it closely. It wasn't the same ring, and it was very poorly made. I couldn't give it to my mother for a present. I sent it back even though I had to pay the shipping costs myself. Then I got an e-mail that said I couldn't get a refund because the time limit was seven days. It said that I could only get a store credit.

I don't think this is right! First, the salesperson gave me the wrong information. Furthermore, the return policy for store purchases is different. In the store, customers have 30 days to get a refund. Finally, I don't need a store credit now because I bought my mother a different birthday present.

I hope that you will send me a full refund. I also think you should tell your clerks to check their information more carefully.

Sincerely,

Beth Weber

Beth Weber

1. The present was for *Beth Weber's mother* ________________.
2. Beth bought ________________________________.
3. She bought it online because ________________________.
4. Beth sent it back because __________________________
____.
5. The time limit for refunds for online purchases was ________________.
6. The time limit for refunds for store purchases was ________________.

Check your answers. See page 140.

2 Number the events in the correct order. Use the information in Exercise 1.

____ She sent the ring back.
____ She didn't like the ring.
__1__ Beth went to the jewelry store to buy a present.
____ The store didn't have the ring in the right size.
____ The company offered her a store credit.
____ She went online.
____ She bought a ring.

3 Complete the sentences.

jewelry	limit	policy	purchase	refund	shipping	store

1. **A** I tried to exchange the coat I bought last week, but the store didn't have the right size.
   B Did the store give you a cash __refund__?
2. **A** I'm going to buy a pair of shoes online.
   B OK. But be sure to ask about the company's refund ________ in case the shoes don't fit.
3. **A** I love to shop online.
   B Not me! When you make a store ________, you can see and touch the things you buy.
4. **A** Sara is really a ________ lover.
   B You're right. She sometimes wears a ring on every finger!
5. **A** The time ________ for returns at Sloan's Department Store is seven days.
   B Wow, that's really short!
6. **A** I got a ________ credit when I returned the necklace I bought.
   B Really? What are you going to buy with it?
7. **A** Are the prices good at the online store that you like?
   B Yes, but you have to pay ________ costs to have the merchandise delivered.

Check your answers. See page 140.

LESSON E Writing

1 Read the paragraph. Complete the outline.

There are several good reasons why I don't usually shop at small neighborhood stores. First, they don't have a very big selection of merchandise. For example, a neighborhood grocery store may only carry one or two kinds of bread, but a big supermarket might have many different choices. Furthermore, small stores don't have the newest merchandise. If you go to a small neighborhood clothing store, they won't always have the latest fashions. Finally, the prices are usually much higher in small stores. Last week, I went into a neighborhood store to find a DVD player, but the price was $ 20 higher than it was in a department store. For all of these reasons, I prefer shopping in bigger stores.

Topic sentence: *There are several good reasons why I don't usually shop at small neighborhood stores.*

Transition 1: ______________

Reason 1: ______________

Example 1: ______________

Transition 2: ______________

Reason 2: ______________

Example 2: ______________

Transition 3: ______________

Reason 3: ______________

Example 3: ______________

Check your answers. See page 140.

2 Complete the outline for a paragraph about why you should shop in small neighborhood stores.

answer all of your questions	give income to people in the neighborhood
finally	often know your name and talk to you
first	only sell the best products
furthermore	second

Topic sentence: *There are several reasons why I like to shop in small neighborhood stores.*

Transition 1: ________ Reason 1: friendly

Example 1: ________

Transition 2: ________ Reason 2: better service

Example 2: ________

Transition 3: ________ Reason 3: better merchandise

Example 3: ________

Transition 4: ________ Reason 4: good for the neighborhood

Example 4: ________

3 Write a paragraph about why you should shop in small neighborhood stores. Use your outline from Exercise 2.

There are several reasons why I like to shop in small neighborhood stores.

____

Check your answers. See page 140.

LESSON F Another view

1 Look at the return-and-refund policy. Then fill in the answers.

Your Best Deal Books

Return-and-Refund Policy

Full refunds:
We will refund 100% of the price for all books and for other new, unopened merchandise that is returned within 30 days. Items should be returned in their original product packaging. You will receive your refund check in six weeks.

Partial refunds:
We will refund less than 100% of the price for:
- any items that are returned after more than 30 days
- any CD, DVD, or video game that is not in its plastic wrapping
- any item not in perfect condition

How to send your return:
1. Call 1-800-555-3132 and ask for a shipping label.
2. Pack the items along with the receipt in a box. You can use the box that the items arrived in or another box.
3. Put the shipping label on the outside of the box.
4. Take the package to the post office.

YourBest DealBooks .com

1. This Web page tells about ____.
   Ⓐ buying merchandise in a store
   Ⓑ returning merchandise to a store
   Ⓒ buying merchandise from an online seller
   ● returning merchandise to an online seller

2. If you don't want a video game that you bought, the first thing you should do is ____.
   Ⓐ call the company
   Ⓑ ask the company for a box
   Ⓒ put the video game in a box
   Ⓓ take the package to the post office

3. You bought a DVD and opened the wrapping. If you return it, you can get ____.
   Ⓐ a different DVD
   Ⓑ all of your money back
   Ⓒ some of your money back
   Ⓓ none of your money back

4. If you get a full refund, the company will send you a refund check in ____.
   Ⓐ ten days
   Ⓑ two weeks
   Ⓒ 30 days
   Ⓓ six weeks

5. You can return ____.
   Ⓐ CDs
   Ⓑ books
   Ⓒ video games
   Ⓓ all of the above

6. Which statement is *not* true?
   Ⓐ You can get a full refund for a book.
   Ⓑ You have to send merchandise back in its original box.
   Ⓒ You need a shipping label to return merchandise.
   Ⓓ You have to send the receipt with the items you are returning.

Check your answers. See page 140.

2 Complete the conversations with a clarifying question.

1. **A** I saw a very cool car parked on Main Street today.
   B Oh, really? What was it?
   A A Talbot Lago. I looked it up online. It's a fancy sports car from 1937. It costs *$300,000!*
   B *It costs how much*?
   And it was parked on Main Street?!

2. **A** Hey, take a look at my new camera.
   B Nice! Where did you buy it?
   A I bought it *at a store in Buffalo*.
   B ____________________?

3. **A** How's your presentation going?
   B Well, I'm working on it.
   A OK, but don't forget. It's due *on Monday*.
   B ____________________?

4. **A** So, Ali, I was walking down the street today and, all of sudden, I saw *Fran*.
   B ____________________?
   A Fran.
   B But I thought Fran was in Hawaii.

5. **A** Our class is going to *go on a field trip* next week.
   B ____________________?
   A Go on a field trip. We're going to the Science Museum.
   B That sounds exciting.

6. **A** I bought *ten* pairs of shoes at TipToe shoe store.
   B ____________________?
   A Ten. They were having a sale.
   B Yes, but you don't need that many shoes!

Check your answers. See page 140.

UNIT 8 Work

LESSON A Listening

1 Listen and complete the letters.

TRACK 26

chart	deal with	initials	share
close up	exhausted	negotiate	work (something) out

Mr. Advice

Dear Mr. Advice,

Marta and I work in a bookstore on the same shift. She runs the cash register and answers questions from customers. I answer the phone and put new books on the shelves. I like Marta, but every afternoon, she calls her children several times on her cell phone. She talks to them for a long time about their day at school. Then they make plans for dinner.

Afternoons are very busy in the store. While Marta is talking to her kids, I have to help the customers, put books on the shelves, and answer the phone – all at the same time. We have a ___chart___ (1) with our duties, and Marta writes her ________ (2) for things that she hasn't done. I'm ________ (3) after work because I'm doing the jobs of two people! She never does her ________ (4) of the work. Sometimes she even leaves early, and I have to ________ (5) the shop by myself. What should I do?

Diana in Denver

Dear Diana in Denver,

First, you should try to ________ (6) with Marta. Explain the problem and agree on a time for one short phone call to her children. Of course Marta wants to know that her children are OK. But work is not the place for long, personal phone conversations.

If she doesn't agree, you should tell your boss, and let him or her ________ (7) the problem. Marta's bad habits will cause problems for the business. But you like Marta and enjoy your job, so I'm sure you can ________ things ________ (8).

Good luck!

Mr. Advice

Check your answers. See page 140.

2 Answer the questions. Use the information in Exercise 1.

1. What are Diana's duties?

   She answers the phone and puts new books on the shelves.

2. What is Diana's problem?

   ____

3. What is Mr. Advice's first solution?

   ____

4. What should Diana do if the first solution doesn't work?

   ____

3 Complete the sentences.

chart	deal with	initials	share
close up	exhausted	negotiate	work (something) out

1. I'm trying to *work* something *out* so I can take the day off tomorrow.
2. I have to stay late because it's my turn to ____________ the store.
3. After you've read this form, please write your ____________ here.
4. When you buy a car, people expect you to ____________ for a better price.
5. Lucy doesn't do her ____________ of the work around here. It's not fair.
6. My boss made a ____________ of the employees' duties and hung it on the wall.
7. I worked for 10 hours today, and now I'm ____________. I don't want to go out.
8. I sometimes have to ____________ difficult customers. It's part of my job.

4 Listen. Then check two true sentences.

TRACK 27

- ☐ Scott sometimes leaves early to go to the library.
- ☐ Scott has asked the owner's permission to leave early.
- ☐ Scott doesn't get paid when Amelia does his work.
- ☐ Jerry thinks that Scott has been irresponsible.

Check your answers. See page 140.

LESSON B Verb tense contrast

Study the grammar explanation on page 131. For a list of past participles, turn to page 134.

1 Complete the chart.

		Present perfect	Present perfect continuous
1.	he / serve	*he has served*	*he has been serving*
2.	they / work		
3.	we / go		
4.	she / help		
5.	I / take		

2 Read the sentences. Circle the correct answers.

1. Diana has been putting books on the shelves for two hours.
   (a.) She's putting books on the shelves now.
   b. All the books are on the shelves.

2. Daria has made strawberry donuts.
   a. We can sell the donuts now.
   b. The donuts aren't ready.
3. Mike has been working as a cashier for two years.
   a. He's a cashier now.
   b. He has a different job now.
4. They have been painting the bookstore.
   a. They finished painting yesterday.
   b. They will finish painting soon.
5. I've been reading that magazine.
   a. I finished reading it.
   b. I haven't finished it yet.
6. I've washed all the dishes.
   a. The dishes are clean.
   b. The dishes will be clean soon.
7. Marta has talked to her kids twice.
   a. She is talking to them now.
   b. She isn't talking to them now.

Check your answers. See page 140.

3 Complete the sentences. Use the present perfect or present perfect continuous. Use *just* where possible.

2:30 p.m.	Diana is already at the bookstore. Marta *has just arrived* (1. arrive) at the store, too. It's very quiet. Only three customers ______ (2. come) into the store so far.
4:00 p.m.	Diana ______ (3. put) books on the shelves for an hour.
5:00 p.m.	The store gets busy. Many people ______ (4. finish) work.
5:30 p.m.	Marta ______ (5. talk) on the phone with her daughter for 20 minutes. Diana is getting angry. She ______ (6. do) Marta's work for nearly half an hour! Suddenly, Marta puts her phone away. Their boss ______ (7. walk) into the store.
7:00 p.m.	Diana's feet are tired. She ______ (8. stand) for five hours.
11:00 p.m.	Diana ______ (9. read) a very funny book that has made her forget her problems. Now she's ready for bed.

4 Read Diana's new schedule. Write sentences about Diana's duties at these times. Use the present perfect or present perfect continuous. Use *just* where possible.

Diana Parker's Work Schedule

2:00 p.m.	Arrive
2:15–3:00 p.m.	Order new books
3:00–4:30 p.m.	Put books on the shelves
4:30–5:00 p.m.	Take a break
5:00–7:30 p.m.	Help Marta at the cash register
7:30–7:45 p.m.	Sweep the floor
7:55 p.m.	Turn off the computer

1. It's 2:05 p.m. *She has just arrived.*
2. It's 2:45 p.m. ______
3. It's 4:00 p.m. ______
4. It's 5:00 p.m. ______
5. It's 5:45 p.m. ______
6. It's 7:59 p.m. ______

Check your answers. See page 140.

LESSON C Participial adjectives

Study the grammar explanation on page 131.

1 Complete the chart.

	Adjectives ending in *-ed*	Adjectives ending in *-ing*
1.	*bored*	boring
2.	frustrated	
3.		exciting
4.	disappointed	
5.		interesting

2 Complete the sentences.

amused	disappointed	frightened	interested
bored	excited	frustrated	relaxed

1. Laila has been reading that book for three hours now. She's underlining sentences in it and taking notes. She's *interested* in the story.
2. Marina has been doing exactly the same thing at work every day for six years. Every day is just like every other day. She's ________________.
3. Tina doesn't like to be alone in her house at night. She's ________________.
4. Eddie and his brother went to the video store, but it was closed, so they couldn't get any videos. They're ________________.
5. Denise just got a much better job with higher pay. She is looking forward to starting next week. She's ________________.
6. Mr. and Mrs. Gray are laughing because their son just told them a very funny story. They're ________________.
7. Rolando had the day off today. He slept a lot, talked to his friends, and watched some TV. He's ________________.
8. Karen has been trying to fix her computer for two hours, but it still doesn't work. She has tried many different things. She's ________________.

Check your answers. See pages 140–141.

3 Circle the correct adjectives.

1. I feel really **tired** / **tiring** this morning because I went to bed very late last night.
2. My co-worker told me an **amused** / **amusing** story about a customer.
3. My job is really **bored** / **boring**. It never changes.
4. Working alone at night is sometimes **frightened** / **frightening**. No other workers are in the building with me, and it's too quiet.
5. Yolanda's boss didn't listen to her complaints, so now she's **frustrated** / **frustrating**.
6. I read an **interested** / **interesting** article about how to get along better with your co-workers.
7. My manager was **disappointed** / **disappointing** in me because I was late to work again.

4 Complete the sentences. Use adjectives ending in *-ed* or *-ing*.

A I hate giving presentations at work! My hands get cold, and my voice sounds strange. I feel really ___frightened___ (1. frighten) when I have to speak to a big group of people.

B Really? Why do you feel scared?

A I'm always afraid my presentation will be ________ (2. bore), and people won't be ________ (3. interest) in it.

B Maybe you could tell a short but ________ (4. amuse) story that will make people laugh.

A That's a good idea.

B And here's another idea. Last week, I saw a great presentation at work. The speaker showed us a few ________ (5. excite) photos. People couldn't believe what they saw!

A OK, I'll bring some pictures. Can you help me prepare my presentation? I can't find the right words, and then I feel ________ (6. frustrate).

B Sure, I can help you! And if you practice a lot, you'll feel more ________ (7. relax).

A But I only have three days.

B Don't worry, you can do it. Your boss won't be ________ (8. disappoint) in you. You're going to give a great presentation!

Check your answers. See page 141.

LESSON D Reading

1 Read. Circle *T* (True) or *F* (False). Then listen.

TRACK 28

The **Soft Skills** That **Employers Want**

To move up in your career, you need two kinds of skills: hard (or technical) skills and soft (or personal) skills. Every job requires different technical skills, but most jobs need the same kinds of soft skills. What soft skills are employers looking for? We asked a group of business leaders this question, and here are their answers.

Good attitude You are happy to be working at this job, and you want to move up in your career. You are interested in your work and want to learn more about it.

Work ethic You show your employer that you will work hard for your paycheck. When you aren't busy, look for another project to do, or help another employee with his or her work. Try to do superb work in all parts of your job.

Teamwork Working well with other employees is very important. You help other people and ask other people for help when you need it. Sometimes your boss won't notice all of the good things that you do, but don't be disappointed.

Confidence You try new things and learn from your experiences. If you make a mistake, correct it as soon as you can. And don't get irritated if your supervisor corrects you. Employers need people who want to try new things.

Communication skills You express your ideas clearly, even if your English isn't always perfect. In most jobs, speaking and writing are equally important. Try to increase your vocabulary by learning at least one new technical word every day. Ask questions if you don't understand things.

People skills You are kind and helpful to your co-workers and to everyone that you meet during your day at work. You know that all people are different, and you try to understand how they feel.

Honesty You are careful with your employer's money and property, and you don't take things home to use for yourself. You repair things if you break them. You don't make personal phone calls or waste time when you're at work.

1. An employee with confidence doesn't need to correct his or her mistakes.	T	F
2. An employee with good people skills understands different kinds of people.	T	F
3. An employee with a good work ethic thinks only about money.	T	F
4. An employee with honesty doesn't read the newspaper during work hours.	T	F
5. An employee with a good attitude is happy to have his or her job.	T	F

Check your answers. See page 141.

2 Write the soft skill that each person has. Use the information in Exercise 1.

	Soft skill
1. Alan always looks for something to work on after he finishes his own work at the donut shop.	work ethic
2. Sharmin really enjoys her job. She wants to get a promotion, so she's taking computer classes after work.	
3. Alexei helped a customer find a great birthday present for her grandmother even though it took a long time.	
4. Young-mi makes salads in the restaurant, but she is ready to learn how to cook. She has offered to help the chefs at lunchtime next week.	
5. Chin worked very hard on the group report even though his name wasn't on it.	
6. Omar waits until his lunch break to call his wife on his cell phone.	
7. Renata is a cashier in a supermarket. She is learning the English names of all the fruits and vegetables in the store so that she can help customers.	

3 Complete the sentences.

automotive equally repair technical
cooperative motorcycle superb

1. To work with all kinds of machines, you need to have strong ___technical___ skills.
2. Jorge speaks excellent English, and he writes __________ well.
3. I want to get a __________ because it's cheaper than a car and a lot more fun.
4. My cousin knows how to __________ computers. He fixed my laptop when it stopped working.
5. My mother is a __________ cook. Everyone loves to come to our house for dinner!
6. Larisa is very __________ with her co-workers. She gets along well with them and always helps them when they are busy.
7. George is studying for a certificate in __________ repair. He wants to work with cars.

Check your answers. See page 141.

LESSON E Writing

1 Read the newspaper ad. Then answer the questions.

HELP WANTED

The Public Library requires a full-time library assistant in the Children's Department. Duties include shelving books, working at the checkout desk, reading stories to young children, and participating in our Homework Helper program after school. You must have experience working with children and communication skills in English and Spanish.

Send resume and cover letter to Eric Russell, Head Librarian, Public Library, 500 Walnut Street, Auburn, KY 42206

1. What is the job? *full-time library assistant* __________
2. Where is the job? __________
3. What are the job duties? __________

   ____
4. What skills and experience should the job candidate have? __________

   ____

2 Read the resume.

Gina Morales
61 Forest Street, Auburn, KY 42206
gm@cup.org ~ (270) 555-4535

Education:
Associate's degree in English, Stone Valley Community College, May 2010

Work experience:
2009–present: Teacher's assistant, 4th grade, Stone Valley Elementary School
2008–2009: After-school math and English tutor, Stone Valley Elementary School

Volunteer experience:
2008–present: "Story Hour" volunteer, Children's Hospital

Skills:
Speak and write English and Spanish fluently

Check your answers. See page 141.

3 Plan a cover letter for Gina. She wants to work at the Public Library. Use the information in Exercises 1 and 2.

1. Today's date: ______________________
2. Inside address
   a. Name and title of addressee: *Eric Russell, Head Librarian*
   b. Address: ______________________
3. Position Gina is applying for:
   a. Job title: ______________________
   b. How Gina found out about the job: ______________________
4. Gina's experience and skills: ______________________

____

4 Write Gina's cover letter. Use your outline in Exercise 3.

Gina Morales

____

____

____

____

____

____

____

______________________:

____

____

____

____

____

____

____

______________________,

____

Check your answers. See page 141.

LESSON F Another view

1 Read the questions. Look at the graph. Then fill in the answers.

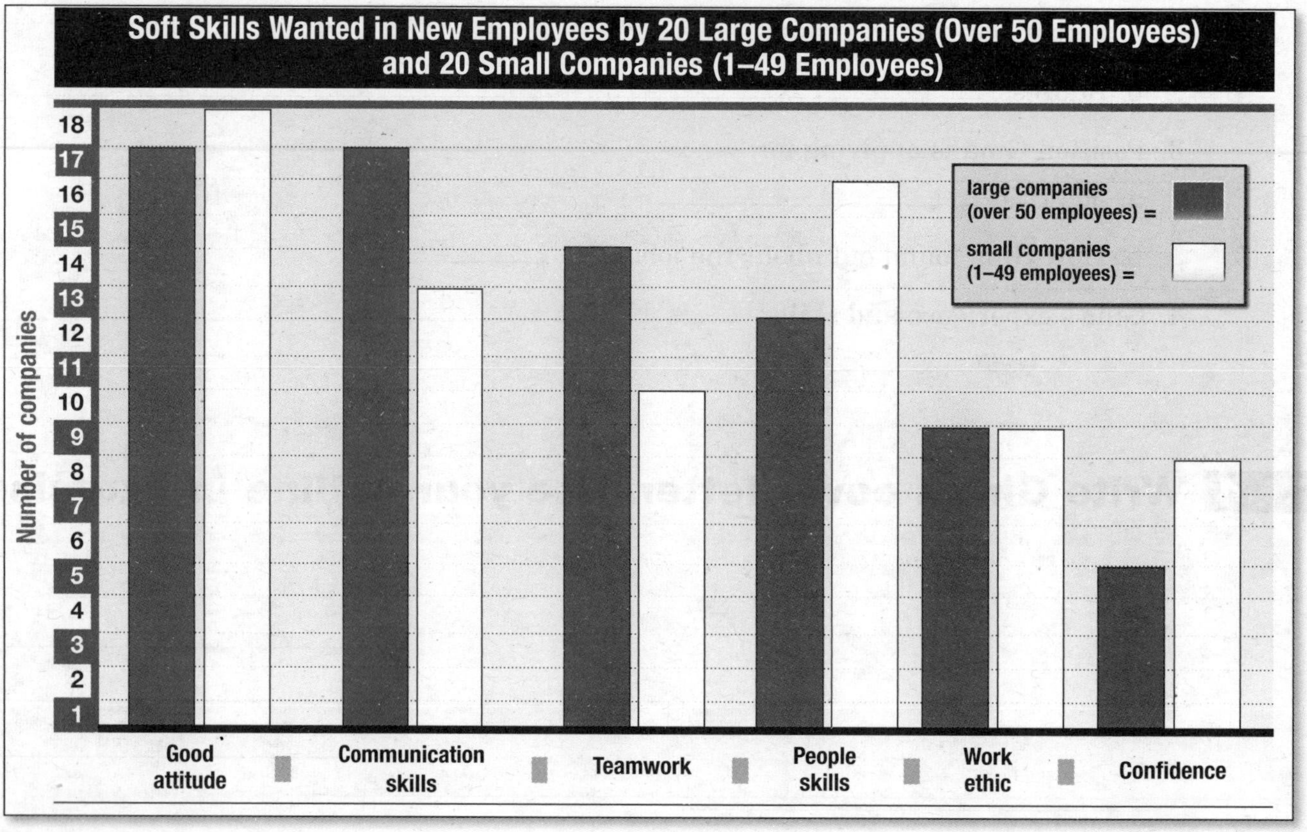

1. This graph identifies ____.
   Ⓐ what soft skills workers have
   Ⓑ how many workers are in each company
   ● what soft skills companies want
   Ⓓ what jobs workers want

2. The information comes from ____.
   Ⓐ 20 companies
   Ⓑ 40 companies
   Ⓒ 49 companies
   Ⓓ over 50 companies

3. What is the most important soft skill for both large and small companies?
   Ⓐ work ethic
   Ⓑ people skills
   Ⓒ good attitude
   Ⓓ teamwork

4. Which soft skill is equally important for both kinds of companies?
   Ⓐ work ethic
   Ⓑ people skills
   Ⓒ teamwork
   Ⓓ confidence

5. Which soft skill is more important at large companies than at small companies?
   Ⓐ confidence
   Ⓑ teamwork
   Ⓒ good attitude
   Ⓓ people skills

6. Which soft skill is more important at small companies than at large companies?
   Ⓐ work ethic
   Ⓑ communication skills
   Ⓒ both a and b
   Ⓓ neither a nor b

Check your answers. See page 141.

2 Choose the best line to complete each conversation.

1. (At the checkout counter in the grocery store)

   A ____? I only have a loaf of bread.

   B No problem. Go ahead.

   A Thanks. I appreciate it.

   (a.) Would you mind letting me go first
   b. May I help you with that

2. (On an airplane)

   A Here, let me help you with that suitcase. It looks pretty heavy.

   B ____.

   A No problem.

   a. Thanks. I appreciate it
   b. I'd be glad to

3. (At the reception desk in an office)

   A Would you let Ms. Caruthers know that I'm here, please?

   B ____. Just one moment.

   A OK. Thanks.

   a. I'd appreciate it
   b. I'd be glad to

4. (At the movie theater)

   A ____?

   B Oh, sorry. I forgot I had it on.

   A Thanks.

   a. Could I please turn off your cell phone
   b. Would you please turn off your cell phone

5. (On the bus)

   A Excuse me, ma'am. ____? I'm getting off at the next stop.

   B Oh, thanks very much. I *am* a little tired.

   A No problem.

   a. Could I take your seat
   b. Why don't you take my seat

Check your answers. See page 141.

UNIT 9 Daily living

LESSON A Listening

1 Read and write the tips. Then listen.

TRACK 29

Buy energy-efficient lightbulbs.
Carpool to work.
Cut down on water use.
Learn about the environment.
Recycle your soda cans.
Replace old appliances.
Take responsibility for your garbage.

Seven Tips to Save the Planet!

1. *Learn about the environment.*
When you know about your effects on the earth, you are more careful about the things that you do every day.

2. ______________________________
Don't drive alone. You'll save money on gas and get to know your co-workers better. And when you aren't driving, you can even sleep a little if you're tired!

3. ______________________________
Take a short shower. Don't run the water while you are brushing your teeth.

4. ______________________________
They are just as bright, and you will save electricity. You can find them at supermarkets and hardware stores for just a few dollars.

5. ______________________________
New refrigerators and stoves are much more efficient. They are expensive to buy, but over time you'll save a lot of money.

6. ______________________________
They're made of aluminum. Making cans from used aluminum uses 95 percent less energy than making cans from new aluminum.

7. ______________________________
Throw things away in the correct place. Some kinds of garbage, like plastic bags, are very dangerous for animals.

Check your answers. See page 141.

2 Cross out the words that are different.

1. appliance	~~lightbulb~~	air conditioner	dishwasher
2. recycle	use again	reuse	throw away
3. reduce	buy more	use less	cut down on
4. carpool	walk	take the bus	drive alone

3 Complete the sentences.

appliances	cut down on	environment	recycle
carpools	energy-efficient	global warming	responsibility

1. The ___environment___ is the air, water, and land around us.
2. Paulo used to drive to work alone every day. Now he ______________ with two of his co-workers.
3. Because of ______________, scientists believe that weather has been changing around the world.
4. We just got a new ______________ air conditioner. It works very well, and it doesn't use much electricity.
5. When you ______________ old bottles, they are made into new glass and used again.
6. The ______________ in my apartment are very old. My landlord doesn't want to buy a new stove or refrigerator.
7. Even though Susan's house has air-conditioning, she uses a fan to ______________ her electric bill.
8. We all have a ______________ to stop pollution and save the earth for our children and our grandchildren.

4 Listen. Then circle the correct answers.

TRACK 30

1. What do Gloria and Ivan talk about changing?
   a. washing machine b. air conditioners c. windows
2. Which is more expensive?
   a. new windows b. a new refrigerator
3. How much would they save if they bought 10 energy-efficient lightbulbs?
   a. $60 b. $50 c. $15

Check your answers. See page 141.

LESSON B Conditional sentences

Study the grammar explanation on page 132.

1 Circle the correct form of the verbs.

1. If I had time, I **will join** / **would join** an environmental club.
2. If you **use** / **used** a fan instead of an air conditioner, you would save electricity.
3. People would buy more energy-efficient lightbulbs if they **are** / **were** cheaper.
4. If you carpooled to work, you **would help** / **helped** reduce global warming.
5. Our city **would be** / **was** cleaner if people recycled more paper and cans.
6. If Rosa **had** / **has** more money, she would buy an energy-efficient refrigerator.

2 Read the sentences. Circle the true statements.

1. If Leon drove more slowly, he would save a lot of gas.
   a. Leon usually drives fast.
   b. Leon usually drives slowly.
2. If we lived outside the city, we would enjoy cleaner air.
   a. We live outside the city now.
   b. We live in the city now.
3. She could save money if she bought recycled paper.
   a. She often buys recycled paper.
   b. She doesn't buy recycled paper.
4. I would be healthier if I rode a bicycle to school.
   a. I don't ride a bicycle to school.
   b. I always ride a bicycle to school.
5. If people recycled all of their paper, we could save a lot of trees.
   a. People recycle all of their paper.
   b. People put a lot of paper in the trash can.
6. If I lived close to my work, I would walk to work.
   a. I live far from my work.
   b. I live close to my work.

Check your answers. See page 141.

3 Write sentences about actions and results. Use the present unreal conditional.

1. Action: I / carpool to work
   Result: I / save a lot of money every week
   If I carpooled to work, I would save a lot of money every week.
2. Action: people / replace old appliances with new appliances
   Result: they / use less electricity
   ____
3. Action: our city / have more recycling centers
   Result: people / recycle more cans and bottles
   ____
4. Action: the landlord / fix the leak in my bathtub
   Result: I / not use so much water
   ____
5. Action: people / use both sides of a piece of paper
   Result: we / not cut down so many trees
   ____

4 Rewrite each sentence a different way. Put the second part of the sentence first.

1. I would buy a more efficient car if I had enough money.
   If I had enough money, I would buy a more efficient car.
2. If we used less gasoline, we would reduce global warming.
   ____
3. You could help save trees if you bought recycled paper.
   ____
4. The beach would be cleaner if people picked up their trash.
   ____
5. If I wore sweaters in winter, I could reduce my heating bills.
   ____
6. If we carpooled to work, we could save money on gas.
   ____

Check your answers. See page 141.

LESSON C Connectors

Study the grammar explanation on page 132.

1 Circle the correct answers.

1. a. There are more people in the city because people are building more houses.
   (b.) There are more people in the city. Therefore, people are building more houses.
2. a. Since the weather is getting warmer, we use more electricity for air conditioning.
   b. We use more electricity for air conditioning, so the weather is getting warmer.
3. a. Because some places have less rainfall, farmers grow less food.
   b. Farmers grow less food. Therefore, some places have less rainfall.
4. a. People are driving bigger cars since they use a lot more gasoline.
   b. Since people are driving bigger cars, they use a lot more gasoline.
5. a. There are more hurricanes now, so living near the ocean is more dangerous.
   b. There are more hurricanes now because living near the ocean is more dangerous.

2 Complete the sentences.

global warming gets worse	they are building more houses
more people want to live outside of cities	they use more gasoline
people have to drive farther to work	

1. Pollution is increasing in the cities, so *more people want to live outside of cities*.
2. Because more people want to live outside of cities, ______________________________.
3. Houses outside of cities are often far from places where people work. Therefore, ______________________________.
4. People who live outside of cities drive more, so ______________________________.
5. Because gasoline use has increased, ______________________________.

Check your answers. See page 141.

3 Complete the chart.

1. warmer weather / global warming / harmful gases
2. air pollution / people get sick / people drive cars
3. places get less rain / global warming / weather patterns change
4. warm ocean water / houses are destroyed / hurricanes are very strong

	Problem	Cause	Effect
1.	*global warming*	*harmful gases*	*warmer weather*
2.			
3.			
4.			

4 Combine or rewrite the sentences. Use connectors.

1. Cause: We recycle only 50 percent of the paper we use.
   Effect: We need a lot of new paper. (since)
   Since we recycle only 50 percent of the paper we use, we need a lot of new paper.
2. Cause: We need a lot of paper.
   Effect: We cut down trees in the mountains. (therefore)
   ______
3. Cause: There aren't as many trees in the mountains.
   Effect: Too much rainwater runs off the mountains. (so)
   ______
4. Cause: Rainwater runs off the mountains.
   Effect: There are terrible floods every year. (since)
   ______
5. Cause: There are floods every year.
   Effect: Many people lose their homes. (so)
   ______
6. Cause: People lose their homes when there are floods.
   Effect: They need a new place to live. (because)
   ______
7. Cause: People need to find new places to live.
   Effect: Animals are losing their natural habitats. (therefore)
   ______

Check your answers. See page 141.

LESSON D Reading

1 Read. Circle *T* (True) or *F* (False). Then listen.

TRACK 31

The Rabbit Problem in Australia

Australia is a very large country with plants and animals that are different from any other place in the world. Until 1859, there were very few rabbits in Australia. In that year, a man named Thomas Austin moved to Australia from England. He liked to hunt rabbits, so he asked his nephew in England to send him 24 healthy English rabbits on a ship. When the rabbits arrived, Austin let the rabbits go on his farm.

Because one rabbit can have 30 to 40 babies in a year and other animals in Australia don't eat the rabbits, the rabbits multiplied very quickly. Soon, there were rabbits all across Australia. By the 1880s, the rabbits were a real problem. Rabbits cause problems because they eat a lot of the plants that farmers grow. They eat too much grass, so other animals have no food. Rabbits also destroy land and kill young trees.

People in Australia have tried many ways to control the rabbits. In 1907, they built a fence that was almost 2,000 miles long to try to stop the rabbits, but it didn't work. In 1950, there were about 600 million rabbits in Australia. Scientists gave the rabbits a disease to reduce the number of rabbits. The disease killed about 500 million rabbits, but by 1991, the number of rabbits had increased again to 200 to 300 million. Now there are fewer rabbits in Australia, but the country still has a serious problem with rabbits – all connected to those 24 rabbits that Thomas Austin brought from England. People today are still furious about what he did.

1. Rabbits first came to Australia in 1907. T F
2. Twenty rabbits came to Australia on a ship. T F
3. A rabbit can have 30 to 40 babies each year. T F
4. Rabbits were a real problem in Australia in the 1850s. T F
5. The Australians built a fence 2,000 miles long to stop the rabbits. T F
6. There were 200 million rabbits in Australia in 1950. T F
7. Rabbits are not a serious problem in Australia now. T F
8. People today are happy about what Thomas Austin did. T F

Check your answers. See page 141.

2 Complete the chart. Use the information in Exercise 1.

Causes of the rabbit problem in Australia	Effects of the rabbit problem in Australia
1. *Thomas Austin brought 24 rabbits to Australia.*	1.
	2.
2.	3.
	4.
3.	

3 Match the antonyms.

1. miserable *d*
2. wise ____
3. summoned ____
4. multiply ____
5. furious ____
6. connected ____

a. calm
b. decrease
c. foolish
d. happy
e. unrelated
f. ignored

4 Complete the sentences.

connected	miserable	peacefully	wise
furious	multiply	summoned	

1. Insects will *multiply* if there are no birds or other animals to eat them.
2. My grandmother is a very ____________ woman who always gives superb advice.
3. A healthy diet and exercise are ____________ with good health.
4. My father was ____________ and shouted at me when I borrowed his car and then got in an accident with it.
5. It was midnight, and everyone in the family was sleeping ____________.
6. Rachel felt ____________ and cried a lot after she failed her exam.
7. The principal ____________ me to her office.

Check your answers. See page 141.

LESSON E Writing

1 Read the paragraph. Then complete the outline.

The Causes and Effects of Littering

Littering means dropping garbage on the ground, and it's a big environmental problem in my city. One cause is that there are not enough trash cans in the streets and parks downtown. We have no good place to throw away papers and wrappers. People don't want to carry their trash home to throw it away. Another cause is that people don't think about littering. They think that one piece of paper isn't important. They see that the street is already dirty, so they drop more litter in it. Because of the litter, the city looks ugly. Since people don't like to go shopping downtown, the stores there lose money. And litter is also expensive because the government has to pay people to clean the streets. If we had more trash cans downtown, I'm sure our downtown would look a lot better, and more people would go shopping there.

Problem: Littering

Causes	Effects
1. *not enough trash cans*	1. ______________
(detail) a. ______________ ______________	2. ______________ ______________
(detail) b. ______________ ______________	3. ______________ ______________
2. ______________	
(detail) a. ______________ ______________	4. ______________ ______________
(detail) b. ______________ ______________	

Check your answers. See page 141.

2 Complete the outline for a paragraph on the causes and effects of water pollution in a lake.

bottles and cans	people throw garbage into the lake
lake is not good for fishing	plastic bags
lake is not good for swimming	water is an ugly color
new factories allow dirty water to go into the lake	water smells bad
people don't want to live by the lake	

Problem: Pollution in our lake

Causes	Effects
1. *new factories allow dirty water to go into the lake*	1. *lake is not good for fishing*
(detail) a. ______	2. ______
(detail) b. ______	3. ______
2. ______	
(detail) a. ______	
(detail) b. ______	

3 Write a paragraph. Use your outline from Exercise 2 to help you.

Causes and Effects of Water Pollution in Our Lake

Pollution is a serious problem in our lake.

____

____

____

____

____

____

____

____

____

____

____

Check your answers. See page 141.

LESSON F Another view

1 Read the questions. Look at the chart. Then fill in the answers.

"In your opinion, what is the most important environmental problem facing the world?" Farmview Community College Student Survey Results		
	1990	Today
Global warming	12%	32%
Energy	16%	19%
Water pollution	18%	13%
Air pollution	19%	12%
Garbage	17%	10%
Loss of plants and animals	7%	7%
City development	6%	5%
No opinion	5%	2%

1. This chart shows ____.
   Ⓐ how the environment will change
   Ⓑ new environmental problems since 1990
   ● students' ideas about the environment in the past and now
   Ⓓ the main causes of environmental problems today

2. In 1990, the largest percentage of students thought ____ was the most important problem.
   Ⓐ energy
   Ⓑ air pollution
   Ⓒ water pollution
   Ⓓ global warming

3. The biggest change between 1990 and today was in the percentage of students who chose ____.
   Ⓐ energy
   Ⓑ garbage
   Ⓒ air pollution
   Ⓓ global warming

4. The percentage of students who chose "loss of plants and animals" in 1990 and today ____.
   Ⓐ went up
   Ⓑ went down
   Ⓒ stayed the same
   Ⓓ was very large

5. Today, students are more worried about ____ than they were in 1990.
   Ⓐ energy
   Ⓑ garbage
   Ⓒ water pollution
   Ⓓ city development

6. In 1990, students were least worried about ____.
   Ⓐ garbage
   Ⓑ global warming
   Ⓒ water pollution
   Ⓓ city development

Check your answers. See page 141.

2 Complete the sentences. Use present real or present unreal conditionals.

1. If people live far from their place of work, they ___spend___ (spend) more money on gas.
2. If we bought an apartment in the city, we ________ (walk) to work.
3. If we remember to turn off the lights, our electric bill always ________ (go down).
4. In our neighborhood, there's usually a flood if we ________ (get) more than six inches of rain.
5. If supermarkets ________ (start) charging for plastic bags, people would bring their own.
6. If you fixed that leaky faucet, you ________ (save) hundreds of gallons of water.
7. If water temperature rises above zero degrees, ice ________ (melt).
8. If we ________ (buy) one of the new lightbulbs, we would save money on electricity.

3 Answer the questions. Use your own ideas.

1. If you had enough money, what would you buy – a new house or a new car?
   If I had enough money, I'd buy a new house.
2. If you went on a long trip, where would you go – around the world or to Antarctica?
   ________.
3. If you are in a fast food restaurant, what do you usually order – a hamburger or a salad?
   ________.
4. If you went on your dream vacation, where would you go – to a beach or to a big city?
   ________.
5. If you are thirsty, what do you drink – water or soda?
   ________.
6. If you need help, who do you usually talk to – your family or a friend?
   ________.

Check your answers. See page 142.

UNIT

10 Free time

LESSON A Listening

1 Read and answer the questions. Then listen.

TRACK 32

To: heather@cup.org
From: nicole@cup.org
Subject: Salma's wedding reception

Hi Heather,

You asked me about Salma's wedding reception. It was wonderful! I didn't know very much about Egyptian wedding customs, so a lot of things really surprised me.

For one thing, Salma and Yusef already had their wedding ceremony last month. Their tradition is to have a very small ceremony for just the parents. Then a few weeks later, they have a big reception for all their friends, family members, and acquaintances.

Another big surprise was that the reception was really two parties, one for men and one for women. The parties were in two different rooms in a hotel. There were 200 women at the party that I went to! I sat at a table with Salma's sisters, and they explained the traditions to me.

After a while, Salma and Yusef came in and sat on a big sofa decorated with flowers. Salma wore a beautiful white dress, and Yusef wore a black suit. We all had a special drink called sharbat that symbolizes good fortune. There was a big show with dancers and musicians, and later we had dinner with a lot of courses. I can't remember all of them!

I was also surprised because guests didn't bring presents to the wedding. Salma and Yusef weren't registered for gifts at a store. Instead, the guests gave money to the bride.

Salma's sister Noora is getting married in October, and she invited me to her wedding reception. I'm really looking forward to it!

Take care!
Nicole

1. What kind of wedding did Salma and Yusef have? an Egyptian wedding
2. What three things surprised Nicole about Salma and Yusef's wedding reception?
____
____
____
3. Who was invited to the ceremony? __________
4. Who was invited to the reception? __________
5. What did people give the bride? __________

Check your answers. See page 142.

2 Circle the correct words.

1. The dinner had three courses. For the first course, we had **soup / coffee**.
2. I love going to wedding receptions because I always enjoy **ceremonies / parties**.
3. A white dress for the bride is a tradition in the United States. It's **a new / an old** custom that many women follow.
4. Mr. and Mrs. Min are acquaintances of my family. We are **very close / not very close** to them.
5. I'm looking forward to my brother's wedding. I'm **happy / not happy** that he's getting married.
6. Grace and Michael are registered for wedding gifts. The store **has / does not have** a list of presents they want.

3 Complete the sentences.

acquaintance	fortune	reception	symbolizes
courses	looking forward	registered	tradition

1. My friends ___registered___ for wedding gifts at Austen's Store.
2. There were more than 300 people at my brother's wedding ________________.
3. The dinner had three ________________: soup, chicken, and cake.
4. It's a ________________ in my culture that the groom shouldn't see the bride's dress before the wedding ceremony.
5. In the United States, brides often wear something borrowed from a happily married family member for good ________________.
6. Throwing rice at a wedding ________________ fertility and longevity.
7. Jorge is ________________ to his graduation party. All of his friends will be there.
8. Dr. Kim is an ________________ of my parents. He lives near them.

4 Listen. Then circle the correct answers.

TRACK 33

1. Giselle and Bill wanted a **small / big** wedding.
2. Giselle's mom **wants / doesn't want** a lot of people at the wedding.
3. For the **groom / bride**, wearing something old symbolizes a connection with the past.
4. Nick thinks that it **is / is not** good to follow wedding traditions.

Check your answers. See page 142.

LESSON B Conditional sentences

Study the grammar explanation on page 132.

1 Decide whether the situations are possible or not possible. Circle the answers.

1. If I had a day off on Saturday, I would go to your graduation party.

   possible   (not possible)

2. We'll buy a wedding present for Clara if we go shopping tomorrow.

   possible   not possible

3. If I had more money, I would take a vacation.

   possible   not possible

4. If Alvaro and Flor weren't so young, they would get married soon.

   possible   not possible

5. If Jason has a birthday party, I'll make a chocolate cake for him.

   possible   not possible

2 Complete the conversation. Use the future real or unreal conditional forms of the verbs.

A I just heard that Mimi and Kwan are getting married in August!

B Really? That's great! If she *invites* (1. invites) me to the reception, I ____________ (2. go).

A I don't know much about Korean weddings. Where do people usually have the reception?

B Well, if they ____________ (3. live) in South Korea, they ____________ (4. have) their reception at a wedding hall. But there are no Korean wedding halls here.

A Mimi is writing the invitations now. If everyone ____________ (5. come), they ____________ (6. have) 200 guests. That's a big wedding!

B Not really. If they ____________ (7. have) their wedding in South Korea, at least 300 people ____________ (8. come)!

Check your answers. See page 142.

3 Andrea is making plans for her birthday party. Write sentences about her real and imaginary plans.

1. Real: weather / be warm / have the party outside

   Imaginary: weather / be cold / have the party in the living room

   If the weather is warm, Andrea will have the party outside.

   If the weather were cold, she would have the party in the living room.

2. Real: her mother / agree / invite 30 people

   Imaginary: her mother / not agree / invite just a few people

   ____

   ____

3. Real: her mother / help her / make decorations for the party

   Imaginary: her mother / not have time to help her / buy decorations at the store

   ____

   ____

4. Real: Andrea / have enough money / buy a new dress

   Imaginary: she / not have enough money / wear her favorite dress

   ____

   ____

5. Real: her friends / have fun at the party / be very happy

   Imaginary: her friends / not enjoy the party / feel bad

   ____

   ____

Check your answers. See page 142.

LESSON C *Hope and wish*

Study the grammar explanation on page 133.

1 Circle the correct words.

1. Jane's wedding is going to be in the park. She really (**hopes**) / **wishes** it won't rain.
2. My grandparents are in China. I **hope / wish** they could come to my graduation ceremony, but they are too old to travel so far.
3. My mother made two cakes for my birthday. I **hope / wish** all my friends will come to my party and eat all this cake!
4. Claudia wants to buy her mother a Mother's Day present, although she doesn't have much money. She **hopes / wishes** she can find something nice that isn't too expensive.
5. I **hope / wish** I could come to your party tonight, but I have a bad cold.

2 Complete the conversation. Use *wish* or *hope* and the correct form of the verb or modal.

A I just got my work schedule for December. I really ___wish___ (1.) I ___could have___ (2. can have) a day off for Christmas! I have to work on the 24th and the 25th.

B Oh, that's too bad. What about New Year's Day?

A We don't have the January schedule yet. I'm not working on December 31st. I ________ (3.) my boss ________ (4. will give) me New Year's Day off, too.

B Well, I'm having a party on New Year's Day, and I am making Mexican food. I really ________ (5.) you ________ (6. can come).

A It sounds like fun! I love Mexican food.

B And I ________ (7.) you ________ (8. will bring) your wife to the party, too.

A You know, I don't like working as a cook in the hospital because I usually have to work on holidays. I ________ (9.) I ________ (10. can find) a better job.

B You should talk to my brother, Antonio. He's a cook in a big restaurant, and he has some holidays off. I ________ (11.) he ________ (12. will be) at my house on New Year's Day.

A Great! I ________ (13.) I ________ (14. can meet) him at your party!

Check your answers. See page 142.

3 Complete the conversations. Write sentences with *I hope*.

1. **A** I can't find my keys! I've looked everywhere.

   B (find / soon) *I hope you find them soon.*

2. **A** I'm not going to class today. I have a cold, and I feel terrible.

   B (feel better / tomorrow) ______________________

3. **A** I'm going to Laura's birthday party tonight.

   B (have / a good time) ______________________

4. **A** I'll see you next week! I'm going to visit my family for three days.

   B (have / a nice visit) ______________________

5. **A** We're going shopping for a wedding present for Maria.

   B (find / great present) ______________________

6. **A** I asked my boss for the day off on Thanksgiving.

   B (get / day off) ______________________

4 Read the situations. Make statements with *hope* or *wish*.

1. Celia wants to buy a perfect present for her friend, but she doesn't have enough money.

   Celia wishes she could buy the perfect present for her friend.

2. I want my parents to visit me on New Year's Eve, but they can't afford to come here.

   ____

3. Keiko wants to have her party outside, but the weather will be too cold.

   ____

4. I want to take the day off on my birthday. My boss said, "Maybe."

   ____

5. Cheng is saving his money to go to his sister's wedding in China.

   ____

6. Denis can't go to the graduation party tomorrow because he's sick.

   ____

7. I plan to take my mother to a restaurant for Mother's Day if I don't have to work.

   ____

Check your answers. See page 142.

LESSON D Reading

1 Scan the article. Write the information. Then listen and read.

TRACK 34

1. the definition of *shower her with presents*
   to give someone many different kinds of presents
2. two examples of things that a mother needs for a new baby
   ______
3. the definition of *crib*
   ______
4. two examples of housewarming presents
   ______
5. the definition of *retiree*
   ______

Parties for Special Times

Americans love to have parties to celebrate transitions in their lives. Three common kinds of parties are the baby shower, the housewarming, and the retirement party.

A baby shower is a party for a woman who is going to have her first baby. The guests are usually all the women friends of the new mother, and they come to her home and "shower" her with (give her many different kinds of) presents. These presents are things that the mother will need for her new baby, such as clothes and toys. If the friends want to buy a big present like a crib (a bed for a baby), they will all give some money and buy the present together. At a baby shower, there is a lot of food, and the women sometimes play games with subjects like baby names. Together, the women celebrate the mother and her baby.

When people move into a new house or apartment, they often have a housewarming party for their family and friends. Sometimes, the housewarming party is the first time that they cook for other people in their kitchen. The guests usually bring a housewarming present for the new home – like a vase or a set of glasses – and they enjoy looking around the new house or apartment.

Another special kind of party is for a retiree, an older person who is going to stop working. Often, the person's co-workers throw a retirement party on his or her last day of work. After work, they have food and music. People make funny speeches and tell stories about the retiree. Sometimes, they give presents like a watch or a photo of all the retiree's co-workers. Then the retiree's boss thanks him or her for many years of hard work.

All of these parties are fun, but they also have a serious significance. They help people mark the important changes in their lives.

Check your answers. See page 142.

2 Write a check (✓) if the sentence is true for each kind of party. Use the information from Exercise 1.

		Baby shower	Housewarming	Retirement party
1.	This party is at home.		✓	
2.	This party celebrates a life change.			
3.	The guests are usually all women.			
4.	The guests are all co-workers.			
5.	People give gifts.			
6.	The guests tell jokes and make speeches.			
7.	There is food.			
8.	The guests look around the house.			

3 Read the sentences. Circle the correct meaning of the underlined words.

1. My parents <u>threw</u> a graduation party for my sister.
   (a.) gave
   b. sent something through the air
2. People who run big companies are often very <u>rich</u>.
   a. they have a lot of money
   b. they have a good sense of humor
3. The <u>object</u> in the museum was made by a Spanish artist.
   a. an important purpose
   b. a physical item
4. I couldn't go to my cousin's wedding because it was too far away and in another <u>state</u>.
   a. a part of a country
   b. a condition of the mind
5. In America, your 21st birthday is a <u>transition</u> from teenager to adult.
   a. a change in conditions
   b. a quick movement

Check your answers. See page 142.

LESSON E Writing

1 Read the paragraph. Then complete the outline.

A Special Indian Holiday

For many Indian people, Diwali is their favorite holiday. The lamps and lights used during Diwali, which is sometimes called the "Festival of Lights," symbolize how good wins over evil.

It is celebrated every year for several days in October or November. On the first day of Diwali, people clean their houses very carefully and decorate them with oil lamps, candles, or electric lights. People also paint colorful pictures on the ground outside their houses. Everyone wears new clothes. Families visit their friends and neighbors and take gifts of flowers and fruit. Some people play cards and other games during Diwali because they believe it will bring good fortune. Indian people love to celebrate Diwali because it is the most colorful holiday of the year.

I. Topic: *A Special Indian Holiday – Diwali*

II. Reason for the holiday: ______________________

III. When it's celebrated: ______________________

IV. Customs:

A. ______________________

B. ______________________

C. ______________________

D. ______________________

E. ______________________

V. Conclusion (why Indian people love this holiday): ______________________

____

Check your answers. See page 142.

2 Complete the outline of a paragraph about the South Korean holiday of Chuseok.

because the whole family is together	to celebrate the harvest and give thanks
eat rice cakes called "songpyon"	visit the tombs of their ancestors (family members who have died)
go to their hometown	wear new clothes
play traditional games	
three days in September or October	

I. Topic: *A Favorite Holiday in South Korea: Chuseok*

II. Reason for the holiday: __________

III. When it's celebrated: __________

IV. Customs:

A. __________

B. __________

C. __________

D. __________

E. __________

V. Conclusion (why South Koreans love this holiday): __________

3 Write a paragraph about Chuseok. Use your outline from Exercise 2 to help you.

Chuseok is a favorite holiday for many people in South Korea.

Check your answers. See page 142.

LESSON F Another view

1 Read the questions. Look at the chart. Then fill in the answers.

What do Americans enjoy doing the most during the November–December holiday season?	Children (under 13)	Teenagers (13–18)	Adults (over 18)
Spending time with family and friends	19%	20%	66%
Going to holiday parties	5%	18%	14%
Watching holiday TV programs and listening to holiday music	20%	5%	8%
Buying presents for other people	1%	8%	2%
Getting presents	55%	49%	10%

1. This chart is about ____.
   Ⓐ Americans' favorite holidays
   Ⓑ people's plans for the holidays
   Ⓒ the presents that most people like to get
   ● what people like to do during the holiday season in the United States.

2. ____ of teenagers say going to holiday parties is their favorite activity.
   Ⓐ Five percent
   Ⓑ Eighteen percent
   Ⓒ Twenty percent
   Ⓓ Twenty-one percent

3. Children's favorite activity is ____.
   Ⓐ getting presents
   Ⓑ going to holiday parties
   Ⓒ spending time with family and friends
   Ⓓ watching holiday TV programs and listening to holiday music

4. Going to holiday parties is most popular with ____.
   Ⓐ children
   Ⓑ teenagers
   Ⓒ adults
   Ⓓ all ages

5. The least popular activity for children and adults is ____.
   Ⓐ getting presents
   Ⓑ going to holiday parties
   Ⓒ buying presents for other people
   Ⓓ watching holiday TV programs and listening to holiday music

6. Compared with children and teenagers, adults are ____ interested in spending time with family and friends.
   Ⓐ more
   Ⓑ less
   Ⓒ as
   Ⓓ not

Check your answers. See page 142.

2 Complete the conversations.

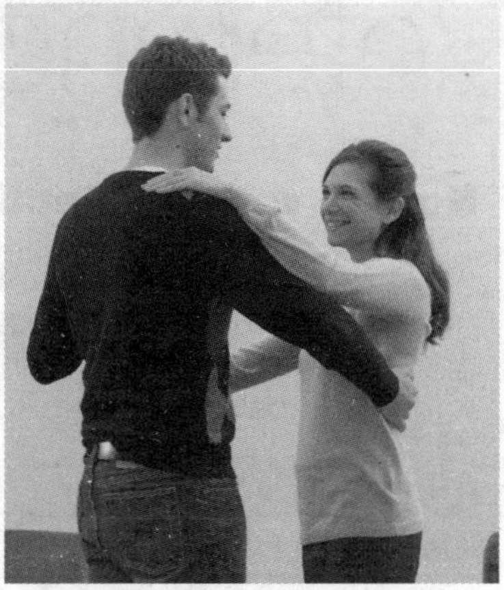

1. **A** You know how to dance the waltz, ___don't you___?
   B Yes, ______________.
   A Can you teach me before the reception tomorrow?
2. **A** Excuse me. We met at Giselle's wedding, ______________?
   B Oh, yes, I remember. You were there with Bill's mom, ______________?
   A No, actually. I'm a friend of Giselle's.
3. **A** The Vietnamese don't usually give presents at a wedding, ______________?
   B No, ______________. They give the bride and groom envelopes with money.
4. **A** Pumpkin pie is a popular dessert for the American Thanksgiving, ______________?
   B Yes, ______________. You tried it at our house last year, ______________?
   A That's right. I did. It was delicious!
5. **A** Tomorrow's a holiday, but Tim has to work, ______________?
   B Yes, ______________, but he's getting a day off next week instead.
6. **A** Luis graduated from college in 2012, ______________?
   B I don't think so. It was in 2011, ______________?
   A Oh, yes. I think you're right.

3 Complete the questions. Then answer *yes* or *no* with true information.

1. You were in high school last year, ___weren't you___?
   ___Yes, I was___. or ___No, I wasn't___.
2. You're studying two languages, ______________?
   ______________.
3. You celebrated your birthday last month, ______________?
   ______________.
4. You're not getting married soon, ______________?
   ______________.
5. You enjoy giving people presents, ______________?
   ______________.

Check your answers. See page 142.

Reference

Nouns, verbs, adjectives, adverbs

Adjectives give information about *nouns*.
Adverbs give information about *verbs*. Most adverbs end in *-ly*.
Adverbs that describe how something happens are called *adverbs of manner*.
A few adverbs are irregular, such as *fast*, *well*, and *hard*.

Adjective + noun	Verb + regular adverb	Verb + irregular adverb
Carol is an *intelligent* girl.	Carol speaks *intelligently*.	Carol speaks *well*.

Sometimes the same word can be an adjective or an adverb.

Adjective	Adverb
It's a *hard* test. John is a *fast* worker.	John works *hard* and *fast*.

Clauses

A *clause* is a part of a sentence that has a subject and a verb.
A *main clause* is a complete sentence.
A *dependent clause* is not a complete sentence; it is connected to a main clause.
A sentence with the structure main clause + dependent clause or dependent clause + main clause is called a *complex sentence*.

that clauses as objects

Some complex sentences have the form main clause + noun clause (see *Clauses* above).
A noun clause is a type of dependent clause. Some noun clauses have the form *that* + subject + verb.
However, it is also correct to omit *that*. The main clause can be a statement or a question.

	Main clause	Noun clause
Statement	People think	(that) she is smart.
Question	Do you think	(that) she is smart?

Present passive

Active sentences have the form subject + verb + object. Passive sentences have the form subject + *be* + past participle. The object of an active sentence becomes the subject of a passive sentence. An active verb is used to say what the subject does. A passive verb is used to say what happens to the subject. A passive sentence is most common when the person or thing that does the action is not important. If the passive is used, and it is important to know who performs an action, a phrase consisting of *by* + noun comes after the passive verb. More often, the passive is used without the *by* phrase.

See page 149 for a list of irregular past participles.

Affirmative statements

Active

The college gives an English placement test twice a year.
The college offers online classes every semester.

Passive

Singular	An English placement test is given (by the college) twice a year.
Plural	Online classes are offered every semester (by the college).

Yes / No questions

Active

Does the college offer financial aid?
Does the college give online courses every semester?

Passive

Singular	Is financial aid offered (by the college)?
Plural	Are online courses given every semester (by the college)?

Wh- questions

Active

When does the college give the placement test?
Where does the college hold English classes?

Passive

Singular	When is the placement test given (by the college)?
Plural	Where are English classes held (by the college)?

Infinitives after passive verbs

Some passive verbs can have an infinitive after them.

Active

The teacher tells the students to bring a dictionary to class.

Passive

The students are told to bring a dictionary to class.

Verbs infinitives often follow

advise	intend	require
allow	mean	tell
encourage	plan	use
expect	prepare	

Direct and indirect questions

A *direct* question is a complete sentence. An *indirect* question contains a main clause and a dependent clause (see *Clauses* on page 126). The main clause can be a statement or a question. If it is a question, a question mark is used at the end of the sentence. The dependent clause in indirect *Wh-* questions begins with a question word (*who*, *what*, *where*, *when*, *why*, or *how*). The dependent clause in indirect *Yes / No* questions begins with *if* or *whether*. *Whether* is more formal.

Wh- questions

	Direct	Indirect
Present	When does the bus come?	Do you know when the bus comes?
Past	Where did she go?	Please tell me where she went.

Yes / No questions

	Direct	Indirect
Present	Do they have a test today?	Do you know if they have a test today? Do you know whether they have a test today?
Past	Did he finish his homework?	I wonder if he finished his homework. I'd like to know whether he finished his homework.

Common introductory clauses that are used with indirect questions

I'd like to know . . .	I wonder . . .	Do you have any idea . . . ?
I don't know . . .	Please explain . . .	Can you tell me . . . ?
I want to know . . .	Tell me . . .	Do you know . . . ?
I need to know . . .		

Present modals: *should, shouldn't, ought to, have to, don't have to*

Ought to is the same as *should*. It is used to give advice. *Shouldn't* is the opposite of both *ought to* and *should*. *Have to / Has to* mean that it is necessary to do something. The subject has no choice about it. *Don't have to / Doesn't have to* mean that it is not necessary to do something. The subject can choose to do it or not.

Affirmative statements

I You We They	should ought to have to	relax.
He She It	should ought to has to	relax.

Negative statements

I You We They	shouldn't don't have to	work so hard.
He She It	shouldn't doesn't have to	work so hard.

Past modals: *should have, shouldn't have*

Should have / shouldn't have + past participle mean that the speaker is sorry about (regrets) something he or she did or did not do in the past. These modals can also be used to give advice about something in the past.

Affirmative statements

<table>
<tr><td>I</td><td rowspan="7">should have</td><td rowspan="7">left earlier.</td></tr>
<tr><td>You</td></tr>
<tr><td>We</td></tr>
<tr><td>They</td></tr>
<tr><td>He</td></tr>
<tr><td>She</td></tr>
<tr><td>It</td></tr>
</table>

Negative statements

<table>
<tr><td>I</td><td rowspan="7">shouldn't have</td><td rowspan="7">arrived late.</td></tr>
<tr><td>You</td></tr>
<tr><td>We</td></tr>
<tr><td>They</td></tr>
<tr><td>He</td></tr>
<tr><td>She</td></tr>
<tr><td>It</td></tr>
</table>

Time clauses with *until* and *as soon as*

Dependent time clauses with *until* and *as soon as* can come at the beginning or end of a sentence.
Use *until* in the dependent clause to say how long an action continues.
Use *as soon as* in the dependent clause to mean "right after."
Use a comma (,) after a time clause when it comes at the beginning of a sentence.

until	*Until* the patient finished his lunch, the nurse stayed with him. The nurse stayed with the patient *until* he finished his lunch.
as soon as	*As soon as* the patient finished his lunch, the nurse left. The nurse left *as soon as* the patient finished his lunch.

Time words and expressions to describe repeated actions

In sentences that talk about repeated actions in the present or past, the correct word order is subject + verb + number of times + time expression.

<table>
<tr><th></th><th></th><th>Number of times</th><th>Time expressions</th></tr>
<tr><td>Present</td><td>This year, Sana volunteers at the shelter
This year, Sana is volunteering</td><td rowspan="3">once
twice
three times
several times
many times</td><td>a week.
each month.</td></tr>
<tr><td>Past</td><td>In 2011, Sana volunteered</td><td>each month.
last year.
two years ago.
when she was 12.</td></tr>
<tr><td>Present perfect</td><td>Sana has volunteered</td><td>so far.
in her life.</td></tr>
</table>

Concession clauses with *although* and *even though*

Although and *even though* introduce dependent clauses of concession. Concession clauses give information that is surprising or unexpected compared to the information in the main clause. Concession clauses can come at the beginning or end of a sentence. Use a comma (,) after a concession clause when it comes at the beginning of a sentence. Usually you can use *but* or *however* to rephrase a sentence with *although* or *even though*, but the grammar is different.

although / even though	*Although / Even though* e-mail is convenient, Mr. Chung doesn't like to use it. Mr. Chung doesn't like to use e-mail *although / even though* it is convenient.
but	E-mail is convenient, *but* Mr. Chung doesn't like to use it.
however	E-mail is convenient. *However*, Mr. Chung doesn't like to use it.

Clauses of reason

Because introduces a dependent clause of reason, which gives reasons for information in the main clause. Clauses of reason can come at the beginning or end of a sentence. Use a comma (,) after a clause of reason when it comes at the beginning of a sentence.

Because wireless technology is fast, many people use it.
Many people use wireless technology *because* it is fast.

Adjective clauses with *who* and *that*

An adjective clause comes after a noun. The noun can be in the middle or at the end of the sentence. It can be a person or a thing. *Who* and *that* are used to describe people. *That* and *which* are used to describe things. There are two kinds of adjective clauses: *subject pattern* and *object pattern*.

Subject-pattern adjective clauses
The adjective clause has the form *who*, *that*, or *which* + verb.
Who, *that*, or *which* is the subject of the adjective clause.

A camera *that is on sale* costs $99.
I want to buy a camera *that costs less than $100*.

The salesperson *who helped me* gave me good advice.
The salesperson *that helped me* gave me good advice.

Object-pattern adjective clauses
The adjective clause has the form *that* + noun or pronoun + verb.
That is the object of the adjective clause. In object-pattern adjective clauses you can omit *that*.

I like the car *that you bought*.
I like the car *you bought*.

The mechanic *that I use* has a lot of experience.

The mechanic *I use* has a lot of experience.

Present perfect

The present perfect is formed by *have / has* + past participle. One of the uses of the present perfect is to talk about recently finished actions (with or without *just*).
See page 134 for a list of irregular past participles.

Affirmative statements

I	have (just)	cleaned the windows.
You		
We		
They		
He	has (just)	
She		
It	has (just)	stopped raining.

Present perfect continuous

The present perfect continuous is formed by *have / has* + *been* + verb *-ing*. Use the present perfect continuous to talk about actions that started in the past, continue to now, and may continue in the future. Use *for* + length of time or *since* + specific time to give the meaning of *how long*.

Affirmative statements

I	have been working	for an hour. since 8:00.
You		
We		
They		
He	has been working	
She		
It		

With verbs that are not actions (e.g., *have*, *be*, *know*), use the present perfect with *for* or *since*:
I have known him for two years. *I have known him since 2012*.
With some action verbs, you can use either the present perfect or the present perfect continuous with *for* or *since*: *I have studied / been studying here for six months*.

Participial adjectives

Verb forms that end in *-ed* or *-ing* are called *participles*. Participles can be adjectives. There is a difference in meaning between the *-ed* and *-ing* forms. Often, the *-ing* form describes a thing or person, and the *-ed* form describes the way someone feels.

Affirmative statements

John's job is very *tiring*. At the end of the day, he is always *tired*. Mary is at the movies. She is *bored* because the movie is very *boring*.

Conditionals

Conditional sentences have a dependent clause and a main clause. The dependent clause begins with *if*. The *if* clause can come at the beginning or end of a sentence. Use a comma (,) after an *if* clause when it comes at the beginning of a sentence. Conditional sentences can be real or unreal. "Real" means the situation in the sentence is possible. "Unreal" means the situation isn't possible; it is imaginary. In unreal conditional sentences, the form of the *be* verb in the dependent clause is *were* for all persons, but in informal situations people use *I was*. The clause *if I were you* is used for giving advice.

Present real conditional

Dependent clause	Main clause	Example
if + subject + present verb	subject + present verb	If you *heat* water to 212° F, it *boils*. Water *boils* if you *heat* it to 212° F.

Future real conditional

Dependent clause	Main clause	Example
if + subject + present verb	subject + future verb	If I *have* time, I *will bake* a cake. I *will bake* a cake if I *have* time.

Present unreal conditional

Dependent clause	Main clause	Example
if + subject + past verb	subject + *would* / *could* / *might* + base form of verb	If I *had* time, I *would bake* a cake. I *would bake* a cake if I *had* time.
if + subject + *were*	subject + *would* / *could* / *might* + base form of verb	If I *were* you, I *would give* Maria a gift card for her birthday. I *would give* Maria a gift card for her birthday if I *were* you.

Connectors of cause and effect

English has many words and phrases to signal cause (reason) and effect (result). Although the meanings of these words and phrases are similar, their form is different.

since and *because*	Use these words in dependent clauses to signal the cause. Use a comma (,) when the dependent clause is at the beginning of a sentence. *Since* / *Because* the earth is getting warmer, the sea level is rising. The sea level is rising *since* / *because* the earth is getting warmer.
so and *therefore*	These words signal an effect. They come at the beginning of a main clause. They are followed by a comma. The earth is getting warmer. *So* / *Therefore*, the sea level is rising.

hope and *wish*

Use *hope* to talk about something you want in the future that is possible. Use *wish* to talk about situations that are not possible (imaginary). Both *hope* and *wish* occur in main clauses and are followed by dependent *that* clauses (see *that* clauses as objects on page 126).

hope	The dependent clause has a present or future verb or modal. I *hope* (that) you *can come* to my wedding. Sandor *hopes* (that) his son *will fly* home for Thanksgiving.
wish	The dependent clause has a past verb or *would* / *could* + base form of the verb. I *wish* (that) you *could come* to my wedding. Sandor *wishes* (that) his son *would fly* home for Thanksgiving.

Spelling rules

Spelling rules for gerunds

- For verbs ending in a vowel-consonant pair, repeat the consonant before adding *-ing*:

  stop → stopping *get → getting*
- For verbs ending in a silent *-e*, drop the *e* before adding *-ing*:

  dance → dancing *exercise → exercising*

  but:

  be → being *see → seeing*

Spelling rules for regular past participles

- To form the past participle of regular verbs, add *-ed* to the base form:
  listen → listened
- For regular verbs ending in a consonant + *-y*, change *y* to *i* and add *-ed*:
  study → studied
- For regular verbs ending in a vowel + *-y*, add *-ed*:
  play → played
- For regular verbs ending in *-e*, add *-d*:
  live → lived

Capitalization rules

Capitalize adjectives that are made from the names of places.	**M**exican girls **I**ranian holiday **A**merican dream
Capitalize important words in titles, but not prepositions or the second part of a hyphenated word.	**S**tory **L**ady **R**unning with **R**opes **M**y **F**avorite **T**ime-saving **D**evice

Irregular verbs

Base form	Simple past	Past participle	Base form	Simple past	Past participle
be	was / were	been	lose	lost	lost
become	became	become	make	made	made
begin	began	begun	meet	met	met
break	broke	broken	oversleep	overslept	overslept
bring	brought	brought	pay	paid	paid
build	built	built	put	put	put
buy	bought	bought	read	read	read
catch	caught	caught	ride	rode	ridden
choose	chose	chosen	run	ran	run
come	came	come	say	said	said
cost	cost	cost	see	saw	seen
cut	cut	cut	sell	sold	sold
do	did	done	send	sent	sent
drink	drank	drunk	set	set	set
drive	drove	driven	show	showed	shown
eat	ate	eaten	sing	sang	sung
fall	fell	fallen	sit	sat	sat
feel	felt	felt	sleep	slept	slept
fight	fought	fought	speak	spoke	spoken
find	found	found	spend	spent	spent
fly	flew	flown	stand	stood	stood
forget	forgot	forgotten	steal	stole	stolen
get	got	gotten / got	swim	swam	swum
give	gave	given	take	took	taken
go	went	gone	teach	taught	taught
have	had	had	tell	told	told
hear	heard	heard	think	thought	thought
hide	hid	hidden	throw	threw	thrown
hit	hit	hit	understand	understood	understood
hold	held	held	wake	woke	woken
hurt	hurt	hurt	wear	wore	worn
keep	kept	kept	win	won	won
know	knew	known	write	wrote	written
leave	left	left			

Answer key

Welcome

Exercise 1 page 2
1. c 2. a 3. c 4. c 5. b 6. a

Exercise 2 page 3
1. stole 6. said
2. was buying 7. left
3. talked 8. was walking
4. spoke 9. saw
5. was standing 10. was looking

Exercise 3 page 3
1. I was reading a mystery when the lights went out.
2. Sue was driving down Park Avenue when she ran out of gas.
3. The fire started when we were watching TV.
4. They were walking past the car when the car alarm went off.
5. The thief stole the bicycle when the boys were playing soccer.

Exercise 4 page 4
1. have, acted 6. forgot
2. have been 7. didn't notice
3. played 8. have, had
4. saw 9. took
5. Have, forgotten 10. needed

Exercise 5 page 5
1. How does Mariah usually get to work?
2. How long does it take her?
3. What was she doing when she heard the news?
4. Why did it take her an hour to get to work?
5. Where did she park?
6. How did she feel at the end of the day?
7. What did she find in her pocket?
8. Where was her car?
9. Has she ever made a mistake like this before?

Unit 1: Personal information

Lesson A: Listening

Exercise 1 page 6
1. aptitude 5. fixing
2. musical 6. mechanical
3. gifted in 7. brain
4. mathematical 8. bright

Exercise 2 page 6
1. F 3. T 5. F 7. F
2. F 4. T 6. T 8. T

Exercise 3 page 7
1. can't 4. good
2. wins 5. can
3. fixing things 6. can

Exercise 4 page 7
1. gifted in 5. musical
2. mathematical 6. mechanical
3. aptitude 7. brain
4. fix 8. bright

Exercise 5 page 7
1. Colin 3. Ruth
2. Ruth 4. Colin

Lesson B: Parts of speech

Exercise 1 page 8
1. perfectly 5. easily
2. quick 6. beautiful
3. skillfully 7. slowly
4. good

Exercise 2 page 8
1. skillfully 4. well
2. beautifully 5. fast
3. hard 6. badly

Exercise 3 page 9
1. professionally 5. carefully
2. skillful 6. wonderful
3. perfectly 7. well
4. slow 8. quickly

Exercise 4 page 9
1. Sita is a slow typist. She types slowly.
Peggy is a quick typist. She types quickly.
2. Sita is a good cook. She cooks well.
Peggy is a bad cook. She cooks badly.
3. Sita is a careful driver. She drives carefully.
Peggy is a skillful driver. She drives skillfully.

Lesson C: Noun clauses

Exercise 1 page 10
1. Alicia's teacher thinks that she is smart.
2. I think that math is an interesting subject.
3. My teacher believes that all her students are gifted.
4. Do you feel that cooking is very important?
5. Do you realize that he'll be famous someday?

Exercise 2 page 10
1. Do you think that people are smart in different ways?
2. Do you agree that exercising three times a week is important?
3. Does your teacher think that you have mechanical aptitude?
4. Do you believe that all children should learn a second language?
5. Do you think that you have an interesting job?
6. Do you feel that all students should take music classes?
7. Does she realize that she is gifted in music?
8. Does he agree that Tom has interesting friends?

Exercise 3 page 11
1. I agree that people are smart in different ways.
2. I'm sure / I'm not sure that women are more interested in taking care of children than men.
3. I feel / I don't feel that mathematical skills are important in life.
4. I believe / I don't believe that men like reading more than women.
5. I agree / I don't agree that women are better at cooking than men.

Exercise 4 page 11
1. I'm sure (that) he's 25.
2. I'd say (that) he's more gifted in music.
3. I think (that) he has an aptitude for singing.
4. I'd say (that) she's 50.
5. I think (that) she's working in an office. / I think (that) she's working at home.

Lesson D: Reading

Exercise 1 page 12
1. f 3. e 5. c 7. h
2. g 4. b 6. d 8. a

Exercise 2 page 12
1. read a book
2. write in a journal
3. do math puzzles
4. work with numbers
5. play the guitar
6. sing with friends
7. draw pictures
8. take pictures
9. dance
10. play basketball
11. help other people
12. join a club
13. spend time alone
14. understand one's own emotions
15. go to a park
16. have a dog or cat

Exercise 3 page 13
1. naturalist 3. visual
2. mathematical 4. interpersonal

Exercise 4 page 13
1. kinesthetic 5. primary
2. multiple 6. Intrapersonal
3. interpersonal 7. visual
4. logical

Lesson E: Writing

Exercise 1 page 14
Paragraph A
1. S 2. T 3. S 4. S
Paragraph B
1. S 2. S 3. S 4. T

Exercise 2 page 14
1. My strongest intelligence is kinesthetic.
2. My primary intelligence is mathematical.

Exercise 3 page 15
Topic sentence:
Victor's primary intelligence is verbal / linguistic.
Supporting details:
He speaks Portuguese, Spanish, and English.
He won first prize in the National Story-writing Contest in 2011.
His hobbies are reading and writing stories.
Victor's mother says: "He could say long sentences before he was two years old!"
Victor's friends say: "He writes really great e-mails!"

Exercise 4 page 15
Answer may vary.

Lesson F: Another view

Exercise 1 page 16
1. C 2. D 3. C 4. A 5. B 6. D

Exercise 2 page 17
1. b 2. a 3. b 4. a

Exercise 3 page 17
1. Yes, I think so. / No, I don't think so.
2. I hope so. / I hope not.
3. I hope so. / I hope not.
4. Yes, I think so. / No, I don't think so.

Unit 2: At school

Lesson A: Listening

Exercise 1 page 18
1. a. She enjoys cooking
b. She likes meeting new people.
2. a. There are seven required classes.
b. There is a three-month required internship in a restaurant.

3. a. She was worried because the program is expensive.
   b. She was worried about her English.
4. a. The counselor said that Kristina qualifies for financial aid.
   b. The counselor said that there are many bilingual students in the program.

Exercise 2 page 19

1. a lot of
2. last
3. can
4. two
5. work
6. must
7. work hard

Exercise 3 page 19

1. industry
2. internship
3. requirement
4. deadline
5. bilingual
6. motivated
7. qualify
8. high-paying

Exercise 4 page 19

1. a math class
2. Sixteen
3. $2,250
4. paid internships

Lesson B: The passive

Exercise 1 page 20

1. is held
2. is offered
3. Is, given
4. are required
5. is, located

Exercise 2 page 20

1. Job placement services are offered by the college.
2. An English test is required by the college.
3. Financial aid is provided by my school.
4. Our homework is checked every night by the teacher.
5. Internships are arranged by the school.

Exercise 3 page 20

1. are held; Passive
2. offers; Active
3. is required; Passive
4. are provided; Passive
5. holds; Active

Exercise 4 page 21

1A. When is Introduction to Food Preparation offered?
1B. It's offered in the fall and spring.
2A. Is a math placement test required for CUAR 102?
2B. Yes, it is.
3A. What time is CUAR 102 offered?
3B. It's offered from 8:00–10:30 a.m.
4A. Where is CUAR 102 held?
4B. It's held in the kitchen in the Anderson Building.
5A. Is Food Safety offered in the fall?
5B. No, it isn't.
6A. Is CUAR 220 offered online?
6B. Yes, it is.
7A. What time is CUAR 220 offered?
7B. It's offered from 8:00–10:30 a.m.

Lesson C: The passive

Exercise 1 page 22

1. (are required) <u>to meet</u>
2. (is asked) <u>to pay</u>
3. (are allowed) <u>to take</u>
4. (is expected) <u>to give</u>
5. (are encouraged) <u>to meet</u>
6. (are told) <u>to work</u>

Exercise 2 page 22

1. New students are expected to come early for registration.
2. All students are required to have a health check-up.
3. Some students are advised to enroll in a math class.
4. Our students are encouraged to visit restaurants.
5. All students are expected to have an internship.
6. Many students are allowed to earn credits for their jobs.
7. Some students are told to go to tutoring.
8. Our students are required to take six courses for the certificate.

Exercise 3 page 23

1A. Are all students required to have an internship?
1B. No, but they are encouraged to get experience in a restaurant.
2A. Are students allowed to earn credit for the internship?
2B. Yes, they are allowed to earn up to five credits.
3A. Are interns expected to work full-time in the restaurant?
3B. No, they are required to work eight to ten hours a week.
4A. Are participants expected to do homework for their internship?
4B. No, they are asked to write a report at the end.
5A. Where are students told to fill out an application?
5B. Students are told to fill out an application online.

Lesson D: Reading

Exercise 1 page 24

1. The story is about Mila, Josif, and Sofie.
2. They moved to Chicago.
3. Josif got a job as a truck driver.
4. Mila wanted a job as a hairstylist.
5. Sofie started school when she was five.
6. Sofie is now 20 years old.

Exercise 2 page 25

1. She left in the 1990s.
2. Mila was a hairstylist, and Josif was a teacher.
3. She couldn't speak English well, and she did not have local work experience.
4. She cut her friends' hair.
5. She bought a salon.
6. Sofie's dream is to become a doctor.

Exercise 3 page 25

1. f 2. d 3. b 4. e 5. a 6. c

Exercise 4 page 25

1. fortunate
2. passion
3. obstacles
4. unstable
5. lacked
6. determined

Lesson E: Writing

Exercise 1 page 26

1. S 2. S 3. O 4. S 5. O 6. S 7. S 8. O

Exercise 2 page 26

1. Mila is planning to open a second salon next year.
2. Mila and her hairstylists all have at least five years of experience cutting, coloring, and styling women's hair.
3. They study fashion magazines every month to get new ideas.
4. She didn't have a job, and she couldn't speak English well.

Exercise 3 page 27

Topic sentence:
Yasmine has several obstacles on her road to success.
Obstacles:
She and her family lost their home in a fire.
She had to start working full-time at age 16.
She couldn't finish high school because she had to work.
Successes:
She was "Employee of the Year" at the Palace Hotel.
She got a GED certificate in 2012.
She received a scholarship to study hotel management at Stone Valley Community College.
Concluding sentence:
She is working hard to achieve her dream of becoming a hotel manager.

Exercise 4 page 27

Answer may vary.

Lesson F: Another view

Exercise 1 page 28

1. C 2. D 3. C 4. B 5. A 6. D

Exercise 2 page 29

1. You're supposed to stop.
2. You aren't supposed to keep driving.
3. You aren't supposed to use the elevator.
4. You're supposed to use the stairs.
5. You're supposed to walk in the pool area.
6. You aren't supposed to run in the pool area.
7. You aren't supposed to use this door.
8. You're supposed to use the other door.
9. You're supposed to turn left.
10. You aren't supposed to go straight ahead.

Exercise 3 page 29

Probable answers:

1. We aren't supposed to go to sleep in class.
2. We're supposed to pay attention.
3. We're supposed to speak English all the time.
4. We're supposed to come to class on time.
5. We aren't supposed to do our science homework in English class.

Unit 3: Friends and family

Lesson A: Listening

Exercise 1 page 30

1. He is grounded for a month.
2. Young-jun's father is angry because he got a C in history.
3. His father wants to raise him the same way he was brought up in South Korea. His father doesn't understand that schools are different in the United States.
4. Young-jun is interested in computers.
5. He wants to talk to Erik about his problem with his dad.

Exercise 2 page 31

1. could
2. a lot of
3. children
4. believe
5. bad

Exercise 3 page 31

1. strict
2. permitted
3. raised
4. grounded
5. chaperone
6. trusts
7. bring up
8. break the rules

Exercise 4 page 31

Anna's mom should talk to other parents with similar problems.

Lesson B: Indirect questions

Exercise 1 page 32

1. direct
2. indirect
3. indirect
4. direct
5. direct
6. indirect

Exercise 2 page 32

1. what grade Young-jun is in?
2. where he goes to school?
3. why his father got so upset.
4. where Young-jun is from?

5. what grades Young-jun got in his other classes.
6. what the history teacher says about Young-jun.

Exercise 3 page 33

1. ?	3. .	5. ?	7. ?
2. .	4. .	6. .	8. ?

Exercise 4 page 33

1. Can you tell me what Young-jun's last name is?
2. Do you know what his address is?
3. Can you tell me what his ID number is?
4. I wonder how many classes he's taking.
5. I want to know who his advisor is.

Lesson C: Indirect questions

Exercise 1 page 34

1. Does Ed live with his parents?
2. Does she have a job?
3. Is there a test next week?
4. Did Lara come to class?
5. Do you have time to help me?
6. Can you go to the party?
7. Why is your mother so strict?

Exercise 2 page 34

1. Can you tell me if she's a new student in our class?
2. Do you know if she is from South Korea?
3. I'd like to know if she's from Beijing.
4. I wonder if she speaks English well.
5. Do you know if she studied English in China?
6. I wonder if she has a job now.

Exercise 3 page 35

1. Can you tell me if we have any homework due tomorrow?
2. I wonder whether you can help me with my homework.
3. Do you know if the bus came?
4. I'd like to know whether I can see the doctor today.
5. Can you tell me if Ms. Ortega is in her office now?
6. Do you know whether Svetlana lives with her parents?

Exercise 4 page 35

1. Can you tell me if you got good grades in high school?
2. I'd like to know whether you had a chaperone on your dates.
3. I'd like to know if your parents were very strict with you.
4. Can you tell me whether you were required to come home before 10:00 p.m.?
5. Can you tell me if you argued with your parents as a teenager?
6. I'd like to know whether your parents liked your friends in high school.

Lesson D: Reading

Exercise 1 page 36

1. He came to the U.S. when he was ten years old.
2. Everything in his life changed.
3. He learned English at work.
4. She stayed at home and took care of Kareem and his brothers.
5. He offered to take care of his brothers so she could study English.
6. She is taking an advanced class now.

Exercise 2 page 37

1. differences	6. success
2. generation	7. create
3. barrier	8. communication
4. immigrants	9. hardships
5. education	

Exercise 3 page 37

1. difference	5. creates
2. successful	6. education
3. immigrants	7. different
4. communicate	

Lesson E: Writing

Exercise 1 page 38

Topic sentence: Marcelo and his parents have very different ideas about ways to communicate.

A. Marcelo: He likes to do everything with his computer.
   1. Example: He always sends e-mails to his friends because it's cheaper and more convenient.
   2. Example: He sends electronic cards with music and funny cartoons.

Transition: On the other hand

B. Marcelo's parents: They like to communicate in more traditional ways.
   1. Example: They always write long letters to their relatives in their home country.
   2. Example: On special days like birthdays, they usually make a phone call, even if it's expensive.

Conclusion: Communicating with friends and family is important to all of them.

Exercise 2 page 39

Topic Sentence: Meena and her daughter, Prita, have very different ideas about clothes.

A. Meena: Meena likes to wear Indian clothes.
   1. Example: Her favorite clothing is a sari. A sari is more traditional.
   2. Example: She likes to buy clothes in India.

Transition: On the other hand

B. Prita: Prita likes to wear American clothes.
   1. Example: Her favorite clothing is jeans and T-shirts. They are more comfortable.
   2. Example: She likes to buy clothes in New York.

Exercise 3 page 39

Answer may vary.

Lesson F: Another view

Exercise 1 page 40

1. C 2. B 3. C 4. D 5. B 6. B

Exercise 2 page 41

1. Manolo said (that) he's been in Boston for two weeks.
2. Manolo told Amelia (that) Boston is a medium-sized city with many different kinds of people.
3. Manolo told Amelia (that) he's living with an American family.
4. Manolo / He told Amelia (that) he's going to teach them to make cheese bread.
5. Manolo / He said (that) the students in the high school are friendly and helpful.
6. Manolo / He said (that) he's going to give a presentation on the history of Brazil next week.

Unit 4: Health

Lesson A: Listening

Exercise 1 page 42

1. She has to work very quickly, and she's afraid of making mistakes.
2. The work is more interesting and less stressful.
3. She feels a lot of anxiety when she takes a test. She can't concentrate.
4. They practice deep breathing and positive thinking.

Exercise 2 page 43

1. calm down, concentrate, cope with stress
2. anxiety, stressed, tense

Exercise 3 page 43

1. tense	5. concentrate
2. breathing	6. calm down
3. stressed	7. meditation
4. anxiety	8. cope with

Exercise 4 page 43

√ taking some deep breaths
√ closing his eyes
√ imagining he was at the beach

Lesson B: Modals

Exercise 1 page 44

1. Advice
   a. Naomi shouldn't spend so much money.
   b. You should look for a better job.
   c. They shouldn't worry so much.
   d. You should eat more vegetables.
2. Necessity
   a. I have to take a computer test.
   b. Alan has to work on Sunday.
3. Lack of necessity
   a. We don't have to take a present.
   b. You don't have to answer the questions.

Exercise 2 page 44

1. have to
2. don't have to, have to
3. have to
4. shouldn't, should
5. shouldn't
6. should
7. shouldn't
8. shouldn't
9. should

Exercise 3 page 45

1. don't have to	4. have to
2. should	5. should
3. has to	6. shouldn't

Exercise 4 page 45

1. I don't have to finish writing this report tonight.
2. You shouldn't find a new place to live.
3. Wilson has to get to work early.
4. You should ask a lot of questions.
5. Risa doesn't have to meditate every day.
6. Teenagers have to follow their parents' advice.

Lesson C: Modals

Exercise 1 page 46

1. shouldn't have	4. shouldn't have
2. should have	5. should have
3. shouldn't have	6. should have

Exercise 2 page 46

1. You shouldn't have slept during class.
2. You shouldn't have forgotten to do your homework.
3. You shouldn't have spoken your native language in class all the time.
4. You should have asked your teacher for help.
5. You should have gone to the tutoring center.
6. You shouldn't have left your textbook at home.
7. You should have kept a vocabulary notebook.
8. You should have practiced English outside of class.

Exercise 3 page 47

1. She shouldn't have overslept.
2. She should have set her alarm.
3. She shouldn't have arrived late for her interview.
4. She should have left her house earlier.
5. She should have asked for directions to the office.

6. She shouldn't have worn jeans for her job interview.
7. She should have gotten more information about the job.
8. She shouldn't have forgotten her briefcase.
9. She should have taken a pen and paper.

Lesson D: Reading

Exercise 1 page 48
1. What is meditation?
2. Where is the best place to meditate?
3. How should I meditate?
4. When should I meditate?
5. How long should I meditate?
6. Why should I meditate?

Exercise 2 page 49
1. thinking seriously about something over a period of time
2. a bedroom
3. your breathing
4. right after getting up or right before bed
5. five minutes
6. 20 minutes
7. helps prevent illness
8. makes you calm in difficult situations, prepares you for positive and negative changes in your life

Exercise 3 page 49
1. meditate 5. loosen
2. regularly 6. nervous
3. Illness 7. react
4. stressful

Exercise 4 page 49
1. ly 3. ion
2. ness 4. ful

Lesson E: Writing

Exercise 1 page 50
1a. action 4a. result
1b. result 4b. action
2a. result 5a. action
2b. action 5b. result
3a. action 6a. result
3b. result 6b. action

Exercise 2 page 50
Topic sentence: I have a lot of anxiety about my job right now.
Action 1: I think about all my problems at work.
Result 1: I can't sleep.
Action 2: I don't sleep enough.
Result 2: I feel tired the next day at work.
Action 3: I can't concentrate.
Result 3: I make mistakes.

Exercise 3 page 51
Topic sentence: I have test anxiety.
Action 1: don't study enough for tests
Result 1: nervous before tests
Action 2: feel tense during tests
Result 2: can't think of the right answers during tests
Action 3: get a bad grade
Result 3: bad grade makes me more nervous about taking tests

Exercise 4 page 51
Answer may vary.

Lesson F: Another view

Exercise 1 page 52
1. D 2. C 3. C 4. A 5. B 6. C

Exercise 2 page 53
1. might, must, might not
2. must, might not, might
3. might, might, must
4. might not, might, must
5. must not, might

Unit 5: Around town

Lesson A: Listening

Exercise 1 page 54
1a. patient
1b. compassionate
2a. She had to talk to the volunteer coordinator at the hospital to get more information.
2b. She had to attend three orientation sessions.
2c. She had to pass some health tests.
3a. She took the toy cart to the children's rooms.
3b. She delivered mail and read cards and letters to the youngest children.
3c. She helped the little children eat their lunch.
3d. She did art projects like drawing and painting with the children.

Exercise 2 page 55
1. want 4. started
2. calm 5. useful
3. live 6. will

Exercise 3 page 55
1. patient 5. can't wait
2. compassionate 6. commitment
3. worthwhile 7. orientation
4. residents 8. coordinator

Exercise 4 page 55
√ take an orientation course
√ promise to work one half day a week

Lesson B: Future time clauses

Exercise 1 page 56
1. as soon as I finish doing mine
2. As soon as I finish cleaning the house
3. until I get home from work
4. until summer vacation ends
5. Until my son eats all his salad

Exercise 2 page 56
1. as soon as 4. until
2. until 5. as soon as
3. As soon as 6. As soon as

Exercise 3 page 57
1. As soon as 4. As soon as
2. as soon as 5. until
3. until

Exercise 4 page 57
1. As soon as Julio arrived at the hospital, he put on his uniform.
2. As soon as Julio got his assignment, he went to Donnie's room.
3. Julio read to Donnie until it was time for the doctor to come.
4. Julio stopped reading as soon as the doctor came in.
5. Julio drew pictures with Donnie until the nurse brought dinner.
6. Julio went home as soon as Donnie finished eating dinner.

Lesson C: Verb tense contrast

Exercise 1 page 58
1. present 4. present perfect
2. past 5. present
3. past 6. present perfect

Exercise 2 page 58
1. a. I volunteer c. I have volunteered
   b. I volunteered
2. a. He begins c. He has begun
   b. He began
3. a. They help c. They have helped
   b. They helped
4. a. I take c. I have taken
   b. I took
5. a. We visit c. We have visited
   b. We visited
6. a. I deliver c. I have delivered
   b. I delivered

Exercise 3 page 58
1. once
2. twice
3. several times
4. many times

Exercise 4 page 59
1. have volunteered
2. volunteer
3. worked
4. give
5. have taken

Exercise 5 page 59
1a. The volunteers gave tours for children eight times last month.
1b. The volunteers have given tours for children twice so far this month.
2a. The volunteers delivered food to the animals 30 times last month.
2b. The volunteers have delivered food to the animals 12 times so far this month.
3a. The volunteers helped in the gift shop 20 times last month.
3b. The volunteers have helped in the gift shop 13 times so far this month.

Lesson D: Reading

Exercise 1 page 60
1a. They had nowhere to go after school.
1b. There was no park in the neighborhood.
1c. Many of the children were home alone without their parents.
2a. Volunteers help the students during "homework hour."
2b. Kids do a computer activity or game.
2c. Each month, they learn about a different topic.
3. The children don't have to participate in any activity if they're not interested.

Exercise 2 page 61
6, 3, 4, 1, 5, 2

Exercise 3 page 61
1. are 5. worried
2. very serious 6. tries hard
3. enjoy 7. proud
4. can't see

Exercise 4 page 61
1. rewarding 5. grave
2. insecure 6. gratifying
3. impaired 7. freedom
4. tenacity

Lesson E: Writing

Exercise 1 page 62
1. Tony made a difference.
2. He visited his grandfather. He played the guitar for him and other people.
3. Tony's grandfather felt bored at the nursing home.
4. He did it in a nursing home.
5. He did it every Saturday while he was in high school.
6. He made the residents of the nursing home happier with his music.

Exercise 2 page 63
1. Susana
2. art projects
3. when she was in college
4. in homeless shelters
5. she loves art and children
6. she helped the children have fun and forget about their problems
7. she works as a teacher

Exercise 3 page 63
Answer may vary.

Lesson F: Another view
Exercise 1 page 64
1. B 2. A 3. D 4. A 5. B 6. C

Exercise 2 page 65
1. used to go, 'm/am not used to traveling
2. didn't use to like, 'm/am used to getting up
3. is used to speaking, used to make
4. used to get, is used to living
5. didn't use to own a car, aren't used to driving
6. used to clean, isn't used to doing

Exercise 3 page 65
Answers will vary.

Exercise 4 page 65
Answers will vary.

Unit 6: Time

Lesson A: Listening

Exercise 1 page 66
1. innovative 5. electronic
2. devices 6. manual
3. convenient 7. distracting
4. text message 8. spam

Exercise 2 page 66
1. F 3. T 5. F
2. F 4. T 6. T

Exercise 3 page 67
1. machine 5. your hands
2. upset 6. off
3. easier 7. computer
4. read 8. new

Exercise 4 page 67
1. innovative 5. text message
2. spam 6. electronic
3. distracting 7. devices
4. manual 8. convenient

Exercise 5 page 67
√ Hank says he doesn't want to spend time commuting.
√ With Hank's teleport machine, people will travel very fast.

Lesson B: Clauses of concession

Exercise 1 page 68
1. d, Although sending e-mail is fast, I think sending a letter is friendlier.
2. c, Even though I have a cell phone, I don't make many calls with it.
3. e, Although I sometimes use a microwave, I think the food doesn't taste good.
4. a, Even though I have a driver's license, I don't own a car.
5. b, Although digital cameras are innovative, I prefer old cameras.
6. f, Even though I don't have air-conditioning, the temperature in my house is comfortable.

Exercise 2 page 68
1. Although David sometimes writes e-mails, he prefers to write letters.
2. Even though David sometimes uses a dishwasher, he prefers to wash the dishes by hand.
3. Although David sometimes gets the news on TV, he prefers the radio.
4. Even though David sometimes uses an air conditioner when it's hot, he prefers a fan.
5. Although David sometimes goes to work in a car, he prefers to use his bicycle.

Exercise 3 page 69
1. Even though Nora has a new cell phone, she likes her old cell phone better.
2. Although I used my GPS, I still couldn't find the way to your house.
3. Although Omar works in an office, he doesn't like to use computers.
4. Even though I sent you three text messages, you never wrote back.
5. Although my mother bought a digital camera, she doesn't know how to take pictures with it.
6. Even though Mr. Cho gets a lot of spam, he likes using e-mail.
7. Although I have a dishwasher, I prefer to wash the dishes by hand.

Exercise 4 page 69
1. Even though I have a microwave, I usually cook on the stove.
2. My camera doesn't work although I put in new batteries.
3. Although his old car often breaks down, he refuses to get a new car.
4. The clothes were too expensive even though the store was having a sale.
5. Even though a plane is faster, I prefer to travel by train.
6. I prefer to use the air conditioner although a fan is cheaper.
7. Even though most people now prefer text messages, I still write e-mails.

Lesson C: Clauses of reason and concession

Exercise 1 page 70
1. b 3. a 5. b 7. b
2. b 4. a 6. b

Exercise 2 page 70
1. Although 4. although
2. although 5. Because
3. because 6. because

Exercise 3 page 71
1. Lisa bakes cakes because it's fun. Although baking cakes is more fun, Linda buys cakes because it's faster.
2. Lisa uses a cell phone because it's convenient. Although cell phones are more convenient, Linda uses a regular phone because it's cheaper.
3. Lisa cooks in a microwave because it's fast. Although cooking in a microwave is faster, Linda cooks in a regular oven because it makes food taste better.
4. Lisa reads the news online because it's quick. Although reading the news online is quicker, Linda reads the newspaper because it's relaxing.
5. Lisa travels by plane because it's comfortable. Although planes are more comfortable, Linda travels by train because it's interesting.
6. Lisa takes lunch to work because it's less expensive. Although taking lunch to work is less expensive, Linda buys lunch because it's easier.

Lesson D: Reading

Exercise 1 page 72
5, 3, 1, 6, 2, 4

Exercise 2 page 73
1. O 3. O 5. O 7. F
2. F 4. F 6. F 8. O

Exercise 3 page 73
1. a lot of 4. wasn't
2. enjoy 5. many
3. not expensive 6. online

Exercise 4 page 73
1. amazing 4. outrageous
2. popular 5. virtual
3. Luckily 6. reasonable

Lesson E: Writing

Exercise 1 page 74
Advantages:
It's very convenient.
I can make calls wherever I am.
It takes pictures.
It's very good in an emergency.
Disadvantages:
My mother calls and talks for an hour when I'm busy.
It's easy to forget at home.
It's easy to lose.
I have to be careful not to break it.
It's hard to understand the instructions.
It takes time to learn how to use it.

Exercise 2 page 75
Advantages: 1. You can find a lot of information on the Internet. 2. You can write e-mails or reports easily. 3. You can learn useful skills for your job. 4. You can play amazing games.
Disadvantages: 1. They cost a lot of money. 2. Computer games make it easy to waste time. 3. You have to spend a lot of time learning to use them.

Exercise 3 page 75
Answer may vary.

Lesson F: Another view

Exercise 1 page 76
1. B 2. A 3. B 4. B 5. A 6. C

Exercise 2 page 77
1. so 5. such
2. such 6. so
3. so 7. such
4. so 8. such

Exercise 3 page 77
1. My Internet connection is so slow that I can't upload photos.
2. I have such an old cell phone that I can't send text messages.
3. Digital cameras are so easy to use that anyone can be a photographer.
4. Many new TVs are so expensive that most people can't afford to buy them.
5. That's such a difficult computer program that no one in the office can understand it.

Unit 7: Shopping

Lesson A: Listening

Exercise 1 page 78
1. He bought a new DVD player.
2. It was too difficult to use.
3. He bought it two weeks ago.
4. Customers can get a refund only if the merchandise is defective.
5. The clerk gave Hassan a store credit.
6. He should always ask about the store policy for refunds and exchanges before he buys anything.

Exercise 2 page 79
1. return 4. a new camera
2. broken 5. the same
3. a different sweater 6. my money back

Exercise 3 page 79
1. exchange 5. refund
2. defective 6. condition
3. warranty 7. merchandise
4. customer service 8. store credit

Exercise 4 page 79
√ The customer wants to see the store manager.

Lesson B: Subject-pattern adjective clauses

Exercise 1 page 80
1. that has a big screen
2. that sells all kinds of computers
3. who helped us
4. that takes good pictures
5. who buy a new cell phone
6. who told me about that store
7. who works in customer service
8. that are in our computer lab

Exercise 2 page 80
1. d, I have a friend who knows a lot about computers.
2. g, I prefer cell phones that have large screens.
3. c, I bought a digital camera that fits in my pocket.
4. f, There are some students in my class who always shop online.
5. a, Maria likes to shop in stores that have good customer service.
6. b, I know a Web site that has great prices on video cameras.
7. e, He loves restaurants that serve Mexican food.

Exercise 3 page 81

1. who / that	5. who / that
2. that	6. who / that
3. that	7. that
4. that	8. who / that

Exercise 4 page 81
1. I wanted to get a microwave that can cook big dinners.
2. I had a microwave that was too small.
3. I went to a department store that was having a big sale.
4. The clerk who / that tried to help me didn't know anything about microwaves.
5. She sold me a microwave that can cook a whole chicken.
6. The microwave that was on sale didn't fit in my kitchen.
7. Another clerk who / that talked to me said that I needed my receipt to return the microwave.
8. I couldn't find the receipt that showed the price of the microwave.
9. I will never shop again at the store that sold me that microwave.

Lesson C: Object-pattern adjective clauses

Exercise 1 page 82
1. The jewelry that she found at a garage sale was very cheap.
2. The jeans that she bought online were not expensive.
3. The jacket that she bought at a secondhand store was only $20.
4. The shoes that she got at a department store were on sale.
5. The blouse that she ordered from a catalog was the wrong color.
6. The dress that she purchased on the Internet was 50 percent off.

Exercise 2 page 82
1. used car that I bought
2. salesperson that we talked to
3. computer that Justin wants
4. camera that my parents gave me
5. the store that you told me about
6. pants that I ordered online
7. birthday present that she received
8. rug that I want
9. coffee table that she likes

Exercise 3 page 83
1. The shoes that she bought on sale are the wrong size.
2. That lamp that she ordered on the Internet is broken.
3. The CD that she found at a secondhand store is scratched.
4. The cell phone that she got yesterday is damaged.
5. The meat that she picked up from the supermarket is spoiled.

Exercise 4 page 83
1. Alan is a student that I met in my English class.
2. The old computer that he always used for his homework suddenly stopped working.
3. The report that Alan is writing is due in three days.
4. The repair shop that he went to couldn't fix his computer.
5. He asked for advice from a neighbor that he knows very well.
6. His neighbor has some old computers that he repaired.
7. Alan bought a computer for only $100 that his neighbor didn't need.

Lesson D: Reading

Exercise 1 page 84
1. Beth Weber's mother
2. a ring
3. the store didn't have her mother's size
4. it wasn't the same ring and it was poorly made
5. seven days
6. 30 days

Exercise 2 page 85
6, 5, 1, 2, 7, 3, 4

Exercise 3 page 85

1. refund	5. limit
2. policy	6. store
3. purchase	7. shipping
4. jewelry	

Lesson E: Writing

Exercise 1 page 86
Topic Sentence: There are several good reasons why I don't usually shop at small neighborhood stores.
Transition 1: First
Reason 1: They don't have a very big selection of merchandise.
Example 1: A neighborhood grocery store may only carry one or two kinds of bread.
Transition 2: Furthermore
Reason 2: Small stores don't have the newest merchandise.
Example 2: A small neighborhood clothing store won't always have the latest fashions.
Transition 3: Finally
Reason 3: The prices are usually much higher in small stores.
Example 3: In a neighborhood store, the price of a DVD player was $20 higher than it was in a department store.

Exercise 2 page 87
Topic sentence: There are several reasons why I like to shop in small neighborhood stores.
Transition 1: first
Example 1: often know your name and talk to you
Transition 2: second
Example 2: answer all of your questions
Transition 3: furthermore
Example 3: only sell the best products
Transition 4: finally
Example 4: give income to people in the neighborhood

Exercise 3 page 87
Answer may vary.

Lesson F: Another view

Exercise 1 page 88
1. D 2. A 3. C 4. D 5. D 6. B

Exercise 2 page 89
1. It costs how much?
2. You bought it where?
3. It's due when?
4. You saw who?
5. You're going to do what?
6. You bought how many?

Unit 8: Work

Lesson A: Listening

Exercise 1 page 90

1. chart	5. close up
2. initials	6. negotiate
3. exhausted	7. deal with
4. share	8. work things out

Exercise 2 page 91
1. She answers the phone and puts the new books on the shelves.
2. Marta doesn't do her share of the work.
3. Diana should negotiate with Marta.
4. Diana should tell her boss and let him or her deal with the problem.

Exercise 3 page 91

1. work, out	5. share
2. close up	6. chart
3. initials	7. exhausted
4. negotiate	8. deal with

Exercise 4 page 91
√ Scott sometimes leaves early to go to the library.
√ Jason thinks that Scott has been irresponsible.

Lesson B: Verb tense contrast

Exercise 1 page 92
1. he has served, he has been serving
2. they have worked, they have been working
3. we have gone, we have been going
4. she has helped, she has been helping
5. I have taken, I have been taking

Exercise 2 page 92
1. a 2. a 3. a 4. b 5. b 6. a 7. b

Exercise 3 page 93
1. has just arrived
2. have come
3. has been putting
4. have just finished
5. has been talking
6. has been doing
7. has just walked
8. has been standing
9. has been reading

Exercise 4 page 93
1. She has just arrived.
2. She has been ordering new books.
3. She has been putting books on the shelves.
4. She has just taken a break.
5. She has been helping Marta at the cash register.
6. She has just turned off the computer.

Lesson C: Participial adjectives

Exercise 1 page 94

1. bored	4. disappointing
2. frustrating	5. interested
3. excited	

Exercise 2 page 94
1. interested 5. excited
2. bored 6. amused
3. frightened 7. relaxed
4. disappointed 8. frustrated

Exercise 3 page 95
1. tired 5. frustrated
2. amusing 6. interesting
3. boring 7. disappointed
4. frightening

Exercise 4 page 95
1. frightened 5. exciting
2. boring 6. frustrated
3. interested 7. relaxed
4. amusing 8. disappointed

Lesson D: Reading

Exercise 1 page 96
1. F 2. T 3. F 4. T 5. T

Exercise 2 page 97
1. work ethic 5. teamwork
2. good attitude 6. honesty
3. people skills 7. communication skills
4. confidence

Exercise 3 page 97
1. technical 5. superb
2. equally 6. cooperative
3. motorcycle 7. automotive
4. repair

Lesson E: Writing

Exercise 1 page 98
1. full-time library assistant
2. in the Children's Department at the Public Library
3. shelving books, working at the checkout desk, reading stories to young children, and participating in the Homework Helper program
4. experience working with children and communication skills in English and Spanish

Exercise 3 page 99
1. Answer will vary.
2. a. Eric Russell, Head Librarian
 b. Public Library, 500 Walnut Street, Auburn, KY 42206
3. a. full-time library assistant
 b. newspaper ad
4. Teacher's assistant for the 4th grade at Stone Valley Elementary School

After-school math and English tutor
"Story Hour" volunteer at children's hospital
Speaks and writes English and Spanish fluently

Exercise 4 page 99
Answer may vary.

Lesson F: Another view

Exercise 1 page 100
1. C 3. C 5. B
2. B 4. A 6. D

Exercise 2 page 101
1. a 3. b 5. b
2. a 4. b

Unit 9: Daily living

Lesson A: Listening

Exercise 1 page 102
1. Learn about the environment.
2. Carpool to work.
3. Cut down on water use.
4. Buy energy-efficient lightbulbs.
5. Replace old appliances.
6. Recycle your soda cans.
7. Take responsibility for your garbage.

Exercise 2 page 103
1. lightbulb
2. throw away
3. buy more
4. drive alone

Exercise 3 page 103
1. environment 5. recycle
2. carpools 6. appliances
3. global warming 7. cut down on
4. energy-efficient 8. responsibility

Exercise 4 page 103
1. a 2. a 3. b

Lesson B: Conditional sentences

Exercise 1 page 104
1. would join 4. would help
2. used 5. would be
3. were 6. had

Exercise 2 page 104
1. a 3. b 5. b
2. b 4. a 6. a

Exercise 3 page 105
1. If I carpooled to work, I would save a lot of money every week.
2. If people replaced old appliances with new appliances, they would use less electricity.
3. If our city had more recycling centers, people would recycle more cans and bottles.
4. If the landlord fixed the leak in my bathtub, I would not use so much water.
5. If people used both sides of a piece of paper, we would not cut down so many trees.

Exercise 4 page 105
1. If I had enough money, I would buy a more efficient car.
2. We would reduce global warming if we used less gasoline.
3. If you bought recycled paper, you could help save trees.
4. If people picked up their trash, the beach would be cleaner.
5. I could reduce my heating bills if I wore sweaters in the winter.
6. We could save money on gas if we carpooled to work.

Lesson C: Connectors

Exercise 1 page 106
1. b 2. a 3. a 4. b 5. a

Exercise 2 page 106
1. more people want to live outside of cities
2. they are building more houses
3. people have to drive farther to work
4. they use more gasoline
5. global warming gets worse

Exercise 3 page 107
1. global warming, harmful gases, warmer weather
2. air pollution, people drive cars, people get sick
3. weather patterns change, global warming, people get less rain
4. hurricanes are very strong, warm ocean water, houses are destroyed

Exercise 4 page 107
1. Since we recycle only 50 percent of the paper we use, we need a lot of new paper.
2. We need a lot of paper. Therefore, we cut down trees in the mountains.
3. There aren't as many trees in the mountains, so too much rainwater runs off the mountains.
4. Since rainwater runs off the mountains, there are terrible floods every year.
5. There are floods every year, so many people lose their homes.
6. Because people lose their homes when there are floods, they need a new place to live.
7. People need to find new places to live. Therefore, animals are losing their natural habitats.

Lesson D: Reading

Exercise 1 page 108
1. F 3. T 5. T 7. F
2. F 4. F 6. F 8. F

Exercise 2 page 109
Causes:
1. Thomas Austin brought 24 rabbits to Australia.
2. Rabbits have 30 to 40 babies a year.
3. Other animals don't eat rabbits, so they multiply quickly.

Effects:
1. Rabbits eat a lot of plants that farmers grow.
2. Rabbits eat too much grass, and other animals have no food.
3. Rabbits destroy land.
4. Rabbits kill young trees.

Exercise 3 page 109
1. d 2. c 3. f 4. b 5. a 6. e

Exercise 4 page 109
1. multiply 5. peacefully
2. wise 6. miserable
3. connected 7. summoned
4. furious

Lesson E: Writing

Exercise 1 page 110
Causes:
1. not enough trash cans
a. no good place to throw away papers and wrappers
b. people don't want to carry their trash home to throw it away
2. people don't think about littering
a. they think one piece of paper isn't important
b. they see the street is dirty, so they drop more litter

Effects:
1. the city looks ugly
2. people don't like to go shopping downtown
3. stores lose money
4. the government has to pay people to clean the streets

Exercise 2 page 111
Causes:
1. new factories allow dirty water to go into the lake
a. water is an ugly color
b. water smells bad
2. people throw garbage into the lake
a. bottles and cans
b. plastic bags

Effects:
1. lake is not good for fishing
2. lake is not good for swimming
3. people don't want to live by the lake

Exercise 3 page 111
Answer may vary.

Lesson F: Another view

Exercise 1 page 112
1. C 2. B 3. D 4. C 5. A 6. D

Exercise 2 page 113

1. spend
2. would walk
3. goes down
4. get
5. started
6. would save
7. melts
8. bought

Exercise 3 page 113

1. If I had enough money, I'd buy a new house. / If had enough money, I'd buy a new car.
2. If I had enough time to go on a long trip, I'd go around the world. / If I had enough time to go on a long trip, I'd go to Antarctica.
3. If I'm in a fast food restaurant, I order a hamburger. / If I'm in a fast food restaurant, I order a salad.
4. If I went on my dream vacation, I'd go to a beautiful beach. / If I went on my dream vacation, I'd go to a big city like Paris.
5. If I'm thirsty, I drink water. / If I'm thirsty, I drink soda.
6. If I need help with a personal problem, I usually talk to my parents. / If I need help with a personal problem, I usually talk to a friend.

Unit 10: Free time

Lesson A: Listening

Exercise 1 page 114

1. an Egyptian wedding
2. The wedding reception was a few weeks after the ceremony. There were two different parties, one for men and one for women. The guests didn't bring presents.
3. the parents
4. friends, family members, and acquaintances
5. money

Exercise 2 page 115

1. soup
2. parties
3. an old
4. not very close
5. happy
6. has

Exercise 3 page 115

1. registered
2. reception
3. courses
4. tradition
5. fortune
6. symbolizes
7. looking forward
8. acquaintance

Exercise 4 page 115

1. small
2. wants
3. bride
4. is

Lesson B: Conditional sentences

Exercise 1 page 116

1. not possible
2. possible
3. not possible
4. not possible
5. possible

Exercise 2 page 116

1. invites
2. will go
3. lived
4. would have
5. comes
6. will have
7. had
8. would come

Exercise 3 page 117

1. If the weather is warm, Andrea will have the party outside. If the weather were cold, she would have the party in the living room.
2. If her mother agrees, Andrea will invite 30 people. If her mother didn't agree, she would invite just a few people.
3. If her mother helps her, she will make decorations for the party. If her mother didn't have time to help her, she would buy decorations at the store.
4. If Andrea has enough money, she will buy a new dress. If Andrea didn't have enough money, she would wear her favorite dress.
5. If her friends have fun at the party, she will be very happy. If her friends didn't enjoy the party, she would feel bad.

Lesson C: Expressing hopes and wishes

Exercise 1 page 118

1. hopes
2. wish
3. hope
4. hopes
5. wish

Exercise 2 page 118

1. wish
2. could have
3. hope
4. will give
5. hope
6. can come
7. hope
8. will bring
9. wish
10. could find
11. hope
12. will be
13. hope
14. can meet

Exercise 3 page 119

1. I hope you find them soon.
2. I hope you feel better tomorrow.
3. I hope you have a good time.
4. I hope you have a nice visit.
5. I hope you find a great present.
6. I hope you get the day off.

Exercise 4 page 119

1. Celia wishes she could buy the perfect wedding present for her friend.
2. I wish my parents could visit me on New Year's Eve.
3. Keiko wishes she could have her party outside.
4. I hope I can take the day off on my birthday.
5. Cheng hopes he can go to his sister's wedding in China.
6. Denis wishes he could go to the graduation party tomorrow.
7. I hope I can take my mother to a restaurant for Mother's Day.

Lesson D: Reading

Exercise 1 page 120

1. to give someone many different kinds of presents
2. clothes and toys
3. a bed for a baby
4. a vase or a set of glasses
5. an older person who has stopped working

Exercise 2 page 121

Baby shower
2, 3, 5, 7
Housewarming
1, 2, 5, 7, 8
Retirement party
2, 4, 6, 7

Exercise 3 page 121

1. a 2. a 3. b 4. a 5. a

Lesson E: Writing

Exercise 1 page 122

I. Topic: A Special Indian Holiday – Diwali
II. Reason: It symbolizes how good wins over evil.
III. When it's celebrated: in October or November
IV. Customs:
A. People clean their houses very carefully and decorate them with oil lamps, candles, or electric lights.
B. People paint colorful pictures on the ground outside their houses.
C. Everyone wears new clothes.
D. Families visit their friends and neighbors and bring gifts of flowers and fruit.
E. People play cards and other games.
V. Conclusion: Diwali is the most colorful holiday of the year.

Exercise 2 page 123

I. Topic: A Favorite Holiday in South Korea: Chuseok
II. Reason: to celebrate the harvest and give thanks
III. When it's celebrated: three days in September or October
IV. Customs:
A. eat rice cakes called "songpyon"
B. go to their hometown
C. play traditional games
D. visit the tombs of their ancestors (family members who have died)
E. wear new clothes
V. Conclusion: because the whole family is together

Exercise 3 page 123

Answers may vary.

Lesson F: Another view

Exercise 1 page 124

1. D 2. B 3. A 4. B 5. C 6. A

Exercise 2 page 125

1. don't you, I do
2. didn't we, weren't you
3. do they, they don't
4. isn't it, it is, didn't you
5. doesn't he, he does
6. didn't he, wasn't it

Exercise 3 page 125

1. weren't you,
Yes, I was. / No, I wasn't.
2. aren't you
Yes, I am. / No, I'm not.
3. didn't you
Yes, I did. / No, I didn't.
4. are you
Yes, I am. / No, I'm not.
5. don't you
Yes, I do. / No, I don't.